FORD MUSTANG

Trivia & Fun Facts Every Fan
Should Know About The Great
American Icon!

By

Dean Harris

ISBN: 978-1-955149-00-6

Please consider writing a review!
Just visit: purplelink.org/review

Have questions? We want to hear from you!
Email us at: dean@purplelink.org

Table of Contents

Introduction 7

Chapter 1: The Birth of An American Icon 9
    Test Your Knowledge! 9
    Fast Facts 15
    Trivia Answers...23

Chapter 2: The Drivers – Key People in the
Mustang's Timeline 27
    Test Your Knowledge! 27
    Fast Facts 34
    Trivia Answers...41

Chapter 3: Running The Numbers 47
    Test Your Knowledge! 47
    Fast Facts 53
    Trivia Answers...59

Chapter 4: The Mustang Over Six Generations 65
    Test Your Knowledge! 65
    Fast Facts 71
    Trivia Answers...77

Chapter 5: Other Wild Ponies 81

    Test Your Knowledge! 81

    Fast Facts 87

    Trivia Answers 97

Chapter 6: The Mustang in Hollywood 103

    Test Your Knowledge! 103

    Fast Facts 109

    Trivia Answers 121

Conclusion 126

Introduction

American car companies are continually striving to innovate changes in how we see, operate, and make connections with cars. The classic car market taps into a simpler time and invokes a feeling of nostalgia. Mustangs are undoubtedly among the most popular classic cars—they were a hit right off the production line, and 56 years later, they still rank among the top-selling cars and are recognized as a household name. Ford's first pony car remains one of the longest-running sports car nameplates in the United States, second only to the Chevy Corvette. The Mustang has set records time and again with its sales, building on its reputation as the classic car that made its way to American homes.

These milestones helped perpetuate the nostalgic standing that draws people to the pony car. The Mustang has left an imprint on the hearts and minds of many Americans, whether it was a memorable first car experience, the project car that brought people together, or memories created while cruising, parking, or doing burn-outs.

It appeals to consumers for other reasons too. At its inception, the Mustang brought a race-care level of performance and speed to the average American. While suburbia was enjoying upward mobility, car lovers were introduced to an affordable sports car that was also easy to work on. Those defining characteristics—accessible, fast, and affordable—continue to shape Ford's marketing strategy to this day.

The Mustang's performance is wrapped up in the ideals of American individualism. A variety of appealing and performance-enhancing trim options from the factory, plus an endless supply of after-market parts, ensure that you can modify and customize to your heart's content. Whether it's the performance you are after, sentiment, or just an affordable sports car, the Ford Mustang surely fits the bill.

The array of Mustangs produced in its lifetime via creative collaborations, advertising promotions, fan-club upgrades, and even Ford's own special projects are too numerous to detail in a single publication. Anyone, from the most fervent enthusiasts to Camaro owners can appreciate this fun collection of Mustang morsels. Or if your intent is to impress your next date or occupy time on the porcelain throne, we hope you enjoy this trivia book!

Chapter 1

The Birth of An American Icon

TEST YOUR KNOWLEDGE!

1. Focus groups were used to narrow in on the Mustang's nameplate; what other name was considered at that time?
   a. Cougar
   b. Torino
   c. T-Bird II
   d. All of the above

2. Commercial production for the Ford Mustang began in what year?
   a. 1962
   b. 1963
   c. 1964
   d. 1965

3. By the time commercial production began, Ford had relied on global distribution to sell their first pony car to consumers around the world.
   a. True
   b. False

4. The first Mustang models available for sale included the hardtop, convertible, and GT.
   a. True
   b. False

5. What other horse logo options did Ford consider before settling on the running Mustang we see today?
   a. A knight on a chessboard
   b. A rearing horse
   c. A Pegasus
   d. A right-facing running horse

6. During the first Mustang production of the 1964 ½ models, how many exterior color options were offered to buyers?
   a. 5
   b. 12
   c. 17
   d. 18

7. What was the Mustang's first most popular color (according to production numbers)?
   a. Rangoon Red
   b. Wimbledon White
   c. Pagoda Green
   d. Vintage Burgundy

8. The "new" 1964 ½ Mustang convertible most closely resembled what other popular Ford vehicle at that time?
   a. Shelby Cobra
   b. Fairlane Sports Coupe
   c. 1963 ½ Falcon Sprint
   d. Sports Roadster Thunderbird

9. The Mustang was the first pony car in the American car market.
   a. True
   b. False

10. What was the Mustang 2+2?
   a. 1962 Mustang I
   b. 1963 Mustang II
   c. 1964 four-seater
   d. 1965 Fastback

11. What was the Mustang's least popular color produced for the 1964 ½ models?
    a. Chantilly Beige
    b. Pace Car White
    c. Champagne Beige
    d. Phoenician Yellow

12. Twilight Turquoise was discontinued once production started for *true* 1965 models and replaced by what popular color?
    a. None, it remained a color option
    b. Tropical Turquoise
    c. Caspian Blue
    d. Skylight Blue

13. How many Mustangs were exhibited at the World's Fair Magic Skyway ride in 1964?
    a. One
    b. Two
    c. Three
    d. Twelve

14. What early milestone Mustangs are in the Henry Ford Museum in Dearborn, Michigan?
    a. Mustang I & Mustang II concept cars and serial number one
    b. Mustang I and Serial Number One
    c. Mustang Serial Number One and the one-millionth Mustang
    d. Mustang I & II concept cars, Mustang Serial Number One, and the one-millionth Mustang

15. Ford produced its one-millionth Mustang in what year?
    a. 1965
    b. 1966
    c. 1967
    d. 1969

16. Other American pony cars, including the Camaro and Firebird, came into direct competition with the Mustang less than a year after the Ford breed was up and running.
    a. True
    b. False

17. The warranty plate paint code *C* in the 1964 ½ model hardtop refers to which color?
    a. Wimbledon White
    b. Honey Gold
    c. Pace Car White
    d. Champagne Beige

18. What popular ABC game show featured the Mustang on the same day it launched on April 17, 1964?
    a. Word For Word
    b. Concentration
    c. Let's Make a Deal
    d. The Price is Right

19. The biggest differences between the 1964 ½ models and 1965 models were purely cosmetic and design changes.
    a. True
    b. False

20. Ford celebrated its first anniversary by adding what two new options to the additional purchase packages offered for new Mustangs?
    a. The Interior Décor Group + The Mustang GT Equipment Group
    b. Pony embossed vinyl upholstery + Thunderbird style door handles
    c. Pony embossed vinyl upholstery + Special Handling Package
    d. Special Handling Package + MUSTANG chromed lettering

CHAPTER 1 FAST FACTS

- The Mustang's origin story includes a number of designs and prototypes that would evolve into two car concepts, the Mustang I and Mustang II, released in 1962 and 1963, respectively. Ford ran an in-house competition to inspire teams to come up with a sporty yet affordable car. Other early prototypes that did not take the same nameplate included the Avventura series, the Allegro series, and a couple of two-seat concept cars, released in 1962 and revisited in 1964. Other early projects that inspired the unibody pony car included the T-5 Project, T-Bird II, XT-Bird, Cougar, Torino, Monte Carlo, and the Fairlane Committee Project. By the time Ford's Mustang II was showcased on October 6, 1963, at the Grand Prix in Watkins Glen, New York, the sports car was a much closer match to what would be commercially available the following year.

- Design changes between the Mustang I and Mustang II were significant. Ford moved from offering a two-seat, aluminum-bodied roadster that resembled an imported sports car more closely to a four-seater with a convertible option. They also realized the impracticality and high cost of mass production of the Mustang I went against Iacocca's goal of making this car an affordable option for American families. In the end, Ford's plants were just not ready to make the innovative Mustang I.

After making its rounds at car shows and automotive events for a couple of years, the design of the mid-engine V4 pony car—standing just under three feet tall and 154.3 inches long with between 90 and 106 horsepower—was set aside as Mustang (but later reintroduced for the GT-40 race car designs). Only two prototypes were built of the Mustang I concept car, and only one was fully functional. It was retired decades later to The Henry Ford Museum in the suburbs of Detroit.

- At Ford, teams were tasked with making the next concept car with as many existing production parts as possible. The Mustang II concept car had a larger steel and fiberglass unibody with more than double of the last design's original horsepower, with a longer wheelbase. The heavier frame allowed for a bigger engine—a front-mounted, High-Performance V8 with 271hp that would later be offered as a special option for production vehicles. Several features, including the 108-inch wheelbase, triple-bar taillights, and purely aesthetic side vents, would be standard in the first production model. Still, only the Mustang II concept car featured a removable hardtop. Only one fully functional vehicle was built (the other was just a design mock-up). After Ford's engineers were done playing with this concept car, it was donated to the Detroit Historical Society in 1975.

- The Mustang was first—officially—offered to American consumers on April 17, 1964. Since Ford used parts already produced at their factories and readily available at dealerships, the pony car had a ticket price of less than $3,000. This put the first-generation model in reach of many Americans, to use either as their weekly grocery getter or an after-hours race car. The same day it was put for sale in dealerships around the United States, Henry Ford II spotlighted the car at the World's Fair in New York.

- Ford started making the Mustang on production lines at its Dearborn, Michigan assembly plant (known as *The Rouge*) on March 9, 1964—a full five months before the typical production cycle, capitalizing on the extra marketing and the attention given to the new model. When August rolled around, they had made enough changes to the production models that the earlier bodies were dubbed the 1964 ½, though Ford officially considers them 1965 models due to their Vehicle Identification Number coding.

- Design and mechanical changes between the 1964 ½ and the *true* 1965 models are numerous but hard to quantify with exactness because components used in early production models sometimes found their way into later 1965 models. This was possibly just to deplete inventories by using what was readily on hand, or maybe as a result of manufacturing the Mustang in assembly plants around the world. In addition to the flagship plant in Dearborn, Ford had made assembly kits for plants in San Jose (California), Edison (New Jersey), Valencia (Venezuela), and Mexico City (Mexico). The most significant difference between these models was the engine size, upgrading the base model's 170 cubic-inch, 101 horsepower engine to the more powerful 200 cubic-inch, 120 horsepower, straight six-cylinder engine. In addition to bigger wheels and more color options, Ford replaced the inferior generator with the industry's latest, new and improved recharging alternator.

- Before the first mass-produced version made it to the assembly lines in March of 1964, marketing teams wanted to demonstrate the power and performance of the Mustang. So they took it to the tracks. The Mustang I was test-driven by Formula One racecar driver, Dan Gurney, at the 1962 Grand Prix, reportedly reaching 120 miles per hour. When the Mustang II was rolled out in 1963, crowds were once again excited to see it at the Grand Prix. In the 1964 Indianapolis 500, the Mustang appeared on the racetrack as a pace car. Later that same year, it raced competitively at the Tour de France Automobile, taking first and second in its touring class and eight and ninth place overall. The Mustang was proving to be every adrenaline-chasing man's race car.

- Even with the global racing spotlights, Ford wanted to do more to reach as many audiences as possible stateside. In the days before the official launch, Ford televised a commercial featuring the Mustang as *The Unexpected*. In it, Ford made an emotional appeal to audiences with its space to seat four, the "elegance of a European touring car," and a variety of additional options as the "the one car that's designed to be designed by you." The ad targeted men and women alike, as carmakers realized the value in marketing to both and sought to increase their consumer base.

- Within a day of its introduction, the Mustang was featured in more than two thousand newspapers from coast to coast, touting its appeal and popularity. Its affordable price tag, sports car performance, and stylish body made the Mustang an immediate hit. Ford's team hoped to sell 100,000 Mustangs in the first year of production. They reached that goal four months after launch. The pony car came out of the gate running as sales only increased after that first year and peaked a full two years later in 1966.

- From the very beginning, Ford's marketing teams came up with winning ways to advertise the Mustang. The early 60s saw Ford's car concepts appear first at the United States Grand Prix in Watkins Glen, New York and later at car shows and automotive events around the country. Ford partnered with J. Walter Thompson advertising agency to maximize their marketing efforts, and together they launched one of the highest volume media campaigns to attract buyers to a new automobile. Other early efforts to promote the Ford Mustang included a giveaway, postcards, a partnership with Holiday Inn to display the car on location and in marketing materials, a new line of sunglasses branded by Mustang, and its presence at events or entertainment venues (including circus and ice performances). Others include airports around the US and abroad, appearances in tv and radio commercials, 30-minute special segments on at least three television networks, a Ford Pavilion Mustang theme ride, and recognition with Tiffany & Co.'s *Excellence in American Design* Award. Not a penny was spared to give the beloved pony car the momentum and attention it deserved from the very beginning. And its popularity since then has only grown.

- Though Iacocca is given most of the credit for naming the Mustang as an executive and general manager of Ford Division at that time, it is not known for sure who came up with the pony car's name. Some sources speculate that John Najjar, an Executive Stylist at Ford, was the first to suggest the name because of his love for the World War II fighter plane, the P-51 Mustang. The fact is that at some point, Robert J. Eggert, Ford Division's Marketing Research Manager, put the name *Mustang* in front of focus groups—inspired by the WW II fighter planes—and it won by a landslide over other proposals.

- The first serialized Mustang, produced sometime in the first few months of 1964, was stamped with a VIN ending in 001. The Wimbledon White convertible was "accidentally sold" three days before the official launch, on April 17, 1964, out of Canadian dealership George Parsons Ford, and purchased by Canadian pilot, Stanley Tucker. When Ford leadership realized what happened, they went to Captain Tucker and asked to buy the pony car back. He declined. However, two years later, when Ford was geared up to produce its one-millionth Mustang, they reached a deal with the pilot. In exchange for the milestone car, Tucker would relinquish serial number one and receive a new Mustang. As a result, the one-millionth Mustang was built to order with every available option from the factory: a 1966 Silver Frost convertible, complete with a black interior, a Philco television, 289-4V engine (it had a better warranty) with 225 horsepower, and a C4 Cruise-O-Matic. Ford acquired the renegade 001, and it is now housed at The Henry Ford museum in Dearborn, Michigan.

- There were only two body styles offered to consumers when production first started: a notchback and a convertible. Of those two 1964 ½ models, the hardtop was the more popular seller. The fastback was rolled out by August of 1964 as another option for the 1965 models. Its more sloped rear window distinguished it compared to the steeper incline of the notchback.

CHAPTER 1 TRIVIA ANSWERS

1. d – All of the above; these were just a few of the prototypes that inspired the pony car.

2. c – 1964; Ford began commercial production in March 1964, a full five months ahead of normal car manufacturing cycles—which is why those early productions are referred to as 1964 ½ models.

3. d – False; First Generation Mustangs were only available for sale in North America. In fact, global distribution didn't occur until the release of its Sixth Generation model in 2015.

4. b – False; Ford only initially offered convertibles and hardtops (or notchbacks). The GT was a performance package rolled out for the first anniversary of the Mustang.

5. a – A knight on a chessboard; the left-facing running horse has had very few changes since its conception. Colors and other elements, including stripes, have been added and removed over the years, but the pony remains steadfast.

6. d – 17; although Ford produced the 1964 ½ Mustang in 18 colors, their *Pace Car White* was only available to dealers and other special giveaways connected to the Indy 500 that year.

7. b – Wimbledon White; this was the most popular Mustang exterior color produced in both the 1964 ½ and the 1965 models, followed closely by the Rangoon

Red. By 1966, Mustang's Candyapple Red surpassed the favorite white's production numbers.

8. c – 1963 ½ Falcon Sprint; a compact two-door (available in hardtop or convertible) with bucket seats and many of the same options as the Falcon, including a 260 cubic inch V8 engine that Mustang used in its 1964 ½ muscle car.

9. b – False; the Plymouth Barracuda rolled off the production floor less than a month before the Ford Mustang. While the Barracuda was released as a fastback coupe with a big engine, the Mustang was described as having the infamous *long hood, short deck* style.

10. d – 1965 Fastback; although the 2+2 was a four-seater available for purchase in September 1964, the model was a 1965 Fastback body style with a fold-down rear seat. Only models offered in 1965 and 1965 featured the unique *Mustang 2+2* emblem.

11. b – Pace Car White; only 190 Mustangs were made in the early production cycles of 1964, and they were all given to very specific groups of people (dealers and elites in the racing world).

12. c – Twelve; in fact, there were three convertibles in four different colors: Raven Black, Wimbledon White, Guardsman Blue, and Rangoon Red.

13. a – None, it remained an option; Twilight Turquoise stayed on the books while Tropical Turquoise became available later in 1964 for the *true* 1965 models.

14. b – Mustang I and Serial Number One; the Mustang II is at the Detroit Historical Society but was brought to The Henry Ford museum in 2014 for a special Motor Muster event celebrating the pony car's 50th anniversary. The one-millionth Mustang is owned by Canadian pilot Stanley Tucker's mechanic and has since fallen off the radar.

15. b – 1966; the one-millionth Mustang was produced and fully loaded with nearly all the options Ford had to offer that year and subsequently given to Canadian pilot, Stanley Tucker, in exchange for his iconic Serial Number One.

16. b – False; the Mustang's nearest competitor at the time of its production was the Barracuda. However, its sales didn't even come close to its Ford counterpart. Chevrolet's Camaro and Pontiac's Firebird didn't even hit the sales floors until late in 1966, and by then the Mustang was dominating the pony car market.

17. c – Pace Car White; only the 1964 ½ models with paint code *C* were Pace Car white. After production changes in the middle of 1964 for the *true* 1965 models, code *C* referred to the Honey Gold exterior paint.

18. d – The Price is Right; the Mustang was featured as an item for contestants to bid on following an announcement the evening before and an advertisement in *TV Guide.* The Mustang was also listed as potential prizes on the other mentioned game shows, which aired on the NBC network.

19. b – False; the biggest change moving into the *true* 1965 models was mechanical. Ford upgraded the engine for base models and extra performance options to add about 20 percent more horsepower to the pony car.

20. a - The Interior Décor Group + The Mustang GT Equipment Group; the Interior Décor Group was also referred to as The Deluxe interior. It was comprised of several unique interior upgrades, including the popular pony-embossed vinyl upholstery. The Mustang GT Equipment Group was rolled out for GT's V8 engines within any selected body style. It offered the four-barrel, 289 cubic-inch engine, and a number of other mechanical and appearance upgrades.

Chapter 2

The Drivers – Key People in the Mustang's Timeline

TEST YOUR KNOWLEDGE!

1. Who was the lead decision-maker at Ford largely credited with bringing the Mustang to fruition?
   a. Lee Iacocca
   b. Carroll Shelby
   c. Stanley Tucker
   d. Henry Ford

2. Which Ford designer sketched the Ford Mustang's earliest creation, capturing the long scoops and soon to be signature louvres?
   a. Eugene Bordinat
   b. Gale Halderman
   c. John Najjar
   d. David Ash

3. What inspired the naming of the *Fairlane* Committee?
   a. Ford's previous model: Fairlane
   b. The charming suburb of Fairlane outside Dearborn, MI
   c. The Fairlane Inn, where planning teams met
   d. J. Walter Thompson's marketing team, in an effort to rebrand the old model

4. What was one of the stipulations Henry Ford required of the Mustang in giving it his full stamp of approval?
   a. It had to sell
   b. One inch of extra backseat legroom
   c. A budget of $45 million
   d. All of the above

5. What market was Iacocca's team primarily targeting with the design and launch of the Mustang?
   a. Baby Boomers
   b. Urban Families
   c. American Workers
   d. Amateur Racers

6. What new technology did Iacocca help bring to the market in the late 90s?
   a. Drones
   b. Electric Vehicles
   c. Electric Bikes
   d. Electronic Gaming Systems

7. Who was the first-ever production owner—via retail purchase—of the Mustang in America?
   a. Gail Brown
   b. Henry Ford II
   c. Stanley Tucker
   d. Harry Phillips

8. Several people involved in Mustang's early years have since been inducted into the Automotive Hall of Fame. Which of the following names has not?
   a. Lee Iacocca
   b. Donald Frey
   c. Hal Sperlich
   d. Carroll Shelby

9. Which Mustang influencer and race car driver was reported to have a heart condition that eventually made him hang up his race helmet?
   a. Henry Ford II
   b. Carroll Shelby
   c. Jack Roush
   d. Buhlie Ford

10. Which Ford Engineer in the 1960s would go on to have a successful, professional racing career and later build special performance Mustangs?
   a. Jack Roush
   b. Steve Saleen
   c. Carroll Shelby
   d. Ken Block

11. What is the name of the vehicle-specific report where you can find detailed information on any Mustang produced between 1967 and 2017?
   a. Standard Marti Report
   b. Deluxe Report
   c. Elite Report
   d. All of the above

12. Who was Ford's Racing Director in the 1960s that helped boost Ford's—and the Mustang's—image with the *Total Performance* campaign?
    a. Carroll Shelby
    b. Dan Gurney
    c. Bud Moore
    d. Jacque Passino

13. What was the nickname given to Steve Saleen on the track?
    a. Gas-Saleen
    b. Shelby Saleen
    c. Saleen 97
    d. Stang Saleen

14. Whose proposal for a more European look led to the most aerodynamic Mustang ever produced in 1979?
    a. Larry Shinoda
    b. Gale Halderman
    c. John Telnack
    d. Bunkie Knudsen

15. Will Boddie led the team that gave us what pivotal new Mustang?
    a. Shelby Cobra
    b. SN95
    c. Boss Mustangs
    d. SN197

16. Who led Ford's *skunkworks* team to save the Mustang?
    a. Alex Trotman
    b. Red Poling
    c. Jackie Stewart
    d. John Coletti

17. Why does the Mustang's pony face left?
    a. Phil Clark was right-handed
    b. The wild mustang symbolically faces *west*
    c. A mirrored copy by John Najjar left it backward
    d. It was the design chosen over the *knight* silhouette

18. What designs were considered to reinvent the fourth-generation Mustang?
    a. The Bruce Jenner
    b. The Arnold Schwarzenegger
    c. The Rambo
    d. All of the above

19. Which Mustang Engineer attended the 1964 World's Fair and led design and development for the first Fifth Generation Mustang?
    a. William Clay Ford, Jr.
    b. Robert Rewey
    c. Art Hyde
    d. Janine Bay

20. Which female Chief Engineer at Ford Motor Company helped lead the first SVT Mustang Cobra development in 1993?

a. Janine Bay

b. Damyanti Gupta

c. Tracie Conn

d. Gail Brown

CHAPTER 2 FAST FACTS

- **The Fairlane Committee**

  It's unclear just how many names were a part of the original Fairlane Committee that met and dreamed up the Mustang. Without a doubt, original members included Lee Iacocca, Donald Frey, Harold Sperlich, Chief Designer Eugene Bordinat, Marketing Executive Frank Zimmerman, Public Relations manager Walter Murphy, and Chase Morsey. As Ford's Car Marketing Manager, Morsey conducted research that concluded that the largest growing car buying group in the 1960s would be between 18 and 34 years old, which included women and families buying a second car. This knowledge would be instrumental in making the Mustang a hit.

- **Lee Iacocca**

  While Henry Ford held the ultimate authority on the Mustang project, Lee Iacocca has been nicknamed the *father of the Mustang*. And it was under his leadership and vision that Ford planning and design teams began brainstorming ideas in secret meetings, away from the prying eyes of Henry Ford and other executives. Recent company failures included the Edsel and an unpopularly upgraded Thunderbird, so Iacocca relied on his marketing team to identify the younger market they wanted to approach with the new *youth car*. By 1961,

Lee's team had decided that the car would need to be affordable, light (for easier handling because women were a part of their target market too), and have the sporty, pony car look with the long hood (which also accommodates a bigger engine). The team also decided that it would have a short deck and be easily customizable with factory options that appealed to as many potential customers as possible. According to Ford's own records, the project was approved by Henry Ford in September 1962, and the rest is Mustang history. Iacocca's contributions to leadership and the automobile industry didn't end there. While still at Ford, he would be later credited with advancing other models, including the Pino, Continental Mark III, Ford Escort, and Mercury's Cougar and Marquis. He even went on to serve as Ford Motor Company's President but was fired in 1978 by Henry Ford II after a series of personal disagreements between the two. Lee was almost immediately hired by Chrysler and worked as the President and CEO until his retirement in the early nineties. Outside of his corporate success, Iacocca's pursuits were various: published author (which included a musical production) and investments across the food/restaurant, real estate development, finance, and gaming industries. His impact on the auto industry was recognized with two awards from the Automotive Hall of Fame and formal induction in 1994.

- **Donald Frey**

  Don was an engineer and Product Planning Manager on the Fairlane Committee but had experience in sales, design, auto safety, and manufacturing. A *Time* article in 1967 described him as "Detroit's sharpest idea man." He sometimes brought work home with him, and in at least one interview, he recounted some brutally honest feedback from his kids that inspired him to start reimagining the cars he was working on. His impact at Ford was significant—he later helped bring disc brakes and radial ply tires to the auto world and worked his way up to Vice President at Ford. He also taught at Northwestern's McCormick School of Engineering, where his reputation as an educator and innovator was valued among students. He created the *Frey Prize* (Margaret and Muir Frey Memorial Prize for Innovation and Creativity, in honor of his parents) to reward undergraduates for ingenuity and creativity. And as an everlasting fan of the Mustang he helped create, Don owned on original two-tone merlot and white 1964 ½ model.

- **Harold Sperlich**

  It was Harold's idea to build the car on the Ford Falcon's chassis. This ultimately saved millions on the production end, as the factory conversions required to build Mustangs where Falcon's had previously been built was both efficient and economical. Ford couldn't afford to devote the financial and other resources to the development of an entirely new car at that time in history. So without this key contribution from the Product Planner, the Mustang very well may have never been born. Another major hit of his: the Chrysler minivan. The engineering genius was inducted into the Automotive Hall of Fame in 2009.

- **Other driving forces** included John Najjar and Philip T. Clark who worked together to design the Ford Mustang I, the earliest prototype. Philip would also later design the Mustang's famous running horse which has largely remained unchanged in its 50+ year continuation. Design credit for the Mustang II is largely given to the Chief Designer and director of Ford's design studio, Joe Oros, and his team of designers: Gale Halderman, Dave Ash, and John B. Foster. Halderman brought in sketches with an Italian styling influence and, with additional input from the rest of the team, the Mustang II concept car took shape. The team worked in the pre-production studio for three weeks, making a prototype that Ford's management would then select as the car that would go on to production. Other designers given credit include Damon C. Woods, Roy Lunn, Herb Misch, Charles Keresztes, and Donald Peterson.
- **Carroll Shelby**
The Mustang was already breaking sales records and Ford's expectations when Carroll Shelby came into Ford

as a consultant. He helped further the pony car's sports car image with the 1966 Shelby Mustang GT350. He and his Shelby American team also transformed Ford's GT racing platform. As a race car driver himself, Carroll Shelby knew what it would take to make the mainstream Mustang into every novice racer's dream. In the 50s, Shelby won a number of awards in professional racing circuits and was recognized as a Driver of the Year two years in a row by *Sports Illustrated.* One of the last and likely greatest racing achievements was his victory in the *24 Hours of Le Mans* in 1959. Shelby didn't partner with Ford again until 2004 when he helped shape Fifth Generation Mustangs. He made a few V6 Shelbys, but because of its superior performance, it came into direct competition with Ford's existing V8, and therefore the project was scrapped. When Shelby GT500's came around again in 2007, the car was made with Shelby's name and blessing but only minimal input by Shelby himself to Ford teams. The automotive giant had many great successes over his long life—the Mustang was just one of them. Mustang lovers can be happy he chose the exciting career in racing over chicken farming.

- **Steve Saleen**
  Saleen won his first race in 1973 in a Shelby Mustang GT350—the second one he owned, after crashing the first—and guaranteed his place in the fast-paced, high-

performance car world. He designed vehicles for years before partnering with Ford Motor Company in 2002. His first contract would be for the legendary race car, Ford's GT40. That contract would later extend to the Mustang and continues into 2021. With Carroll Shelby beside him in 1996, Steve Saleen was inducted into the Mustang Hall of Fame.

- **Kevin Marti**

  Contracted as the only licensee to hold Ford Motor Company's entire North American production database from 1967 to 2017, Kevin Marti acknowledges how privileged he feels to be in that unique position. His company, Marti Auto Works, started as a hobby of restoring Mustangs and Cougars. When he ran into issues trying to find the parts he needed, he decided to use his own skills and background as an engineer, plus a growing network of technicians, machinists, and engineers to make reproduction parts. Marti eventually built a relationship with decision-makers at Ford Motor Company that opened the door for other opportunities, including the purchase of obsolete original parts, original Ford invoices, and the contract to license Ford's database covering every serial number produced over 50 years. He has since used all his resources to write a few books that include thousands of production statistics for both the Mustang and the Cougar, and the *Tagbook* which illustrates all the different tags that Ford has used for those two models. For Mustang owners looking to discover original information on their own vehicle, Kevin Marti's wealth of personal knowledge, contacts, and authentic information are invaluable.

CHAPTER 2 TRIVIA ANSWERS

1. a – Lee Iacocca; as the Ford Division's Vice President and General Manager in the early 1960s, Iacocca led teams in Dearborn through the development of the Mustang.
2. b – Gale Halderman; he was a part of the original design team that brainstormed ideas for Iacocca's vision in the early 1960s.
3. c – The Fairlane Inn, where planning teams met; since senior Ford leadership met at the Dearborn Inn, Iacocca wanted a different place for his team to work, outside of headquarters and the influence of other managers and decision-makers.
4. d – All of the above; money was tight at Ford because of the recent $250 million loss on the Edsel, so Henry Ford cut Iacocca's requested budget by $30 million. Even so, Ford was hoping that Iacocca's four-seater pony car project would save them from further disaster.
5. a – Baby Boomers; research recognized the buying power this generation had as it settled in post-WWII with fortuitous timing.
6. c – Electric Bikes; Iacocca helped found and later ran EV Global Motors, rolling out the E-Bike SX, one of the first popular electric bicycles in the United States.
7. a – Gail Brown; Gail purchased the production Skylight Blue convertible in Chicago on April 15, 1964—a full two days before the vehicle was supposed to be for sale.

While Stanley Tucker bought Serial Number One three days before Mustangs went public, the transaction—aided by salesman, Harry Phillips—took place in Canada, the Mustang didn't leave the dealership until the 17th, *and* that particular pre-production Mustang was never meant for retail sale.

8. b – Donald Frey; as an accomplished engineer and teacher, Frey made an impact on educating and promoting new ideas—and not just in the automotive world.

9. b – Carroll Shelby; despite suffering from a heart condition from an early age, Shelby didn't let his health slow him down. Toward the end of his racing career, he was reportedly taking nitroglycerin tablets to keep his heart going. He received a heart transplant, a kidney transplant, married seven times, and fathered three children over his lifetime, and still managed to live until the age of 89.

10. a – Jack Roush; Jack's career in the automotive world began in 1964 at Ford where he developed engines. He used his engineering expertise to open his own company in 1976, making engines and other parts for high-performance cars and boats. He would go on to compete professionally in drag racing and NASCAR events around the world claiming many championships. The man must have a soft spot for Mustangs because he has upgraded over 16,000 Ford pony cars with his specialized performance packages and improvements.

11. d – All of the above; with the Marti Report, buyers can order several different versions that include more comprehensive information about the vehicle's history from Ford's own database. The Standard, Deluxe, or Elite Reports offer everything from factory options and statistics specific to a car, factory and assembly line data, door data plate information, personalized production statistics, to reproductions of the door data plate and window sticker for the most eager hobbyist.

12. d - Jacque Passino; Ford's Racing Director was enlisted to bring performance potential to the Mustang's sporty design. With Passino's help and collaboration with greats like Shelby, Ford created a number of models in the 1970s that met the *race car* standards.

13. a – Gas-Saleen; Steve took first place at the Riverside International Raceway in 1973, gaining his speed and performance reputation. Fellow racers gave him the nickname sometime after he moved into the Formula Atlantic race series.

14. c – John Telnack; John J. "Jack" Telnack, also a Mustang Hall of Fame inductee, worked for Joe Oros and helped come up with some fastback designs for the Mustang. After returning from Ford of Europe's design department, Telnack came up with a more sleek European-looking design for the 1979 model Mustang. The more aerodynamic styling was a hit, and he was later promoted to Ford's Global Vice President of

Design, producing hits that included the 1983 Thunderbird and 1986 Taurus.

15. b – SN95; Will Boddie led Ford Motor Company in the Mustang's new direction as Director for Small & Mid-sized cars.

16. d – John Coletti; the *skunkworks* team would eventually become Team Mustang, but Coletti led around 75 people over the course of three years to develop the new Mustang and revive Ford's legacy.

17. a - Phil Clark was right-handed; there's no secret behind the left facing pony. As a member of the early design team for the Mustang I concept car, Philip Clark came forward with his rendition of the mustang that the team had settled on as a name. Since he was right-handed, he naturally drew from left to right. Later, Iacocca was quoted as saying, "the Mustang is a wild horse, not a domesticated racer" in reference to why the horse didn't face right, the direction horses ran on a track.

18. d – All of the above; The names were a reflection of the design concept for the 1994 models being proposed. The Arnold Schwarzenegger—broad-shouldered, muscular, and aerodynamic body—won the face of development.

19. c – Art Hyde; though he was still in elementary school when he attended the 1964 World's Fair, Hyde said it left an impression that would carry him into Ford for his first interview in the 70s. His goal of becoming Chief

Program Engineer for the Mustang would come to fruition in 1998 and last until 2001.

20. a – Janine Bay; Janine was Chief Program Engineer for the Mustang for almost two years, from January 1997 – August 1998. She also worked as a vehicle line director and under John Coletti's leadership on the Special Vehicle Team.

Chapter 3

Running The Numbers

1. What year did the Mustang sell the most cars?
   a. 1965
   b. 1966
   c. 1967
   d. 1979

2. How much did Bob Kiernan pay for the 1968 Highland Green *Bullitt* Mustang, when he purchased it in 1974?
   a. $7,400
   b. $5,300
   c. $3,500
   d. $2,300

3. What was Ford's heaviest Mustang body?
   a. 2003 Cobra Convertible
   b. 2007 GT500 Convertible
   c. 2008 GT500KR
   d. 2011 GT500 Coupe

4. What Mustang body had the lightest curb weight?
   a. 1965 Hardtop
   b. 1979 Hatchback
   c. 1979 Coupe
   d. 1981 Cobra

5. Which famous Ford Mustang was inducted—as the only Mustang—into the National Historic Vehicle Register?
   a. Bond (Sean Connery) Mustang
   b. Ford's Serial Number One
   c. 1968 *Bullitt*
   d. Ford's last 1995 5.0

6. What year did the Mustang win *Motor Trend's* "Car of the Year" award?
   a. 1968
   b. 1974
   c. 1994
   d. b & c

7. The *Fox-Body* platform was used across the entire Fourth & Fifth Generation Mustangs, from 1979 to 2004.
    a. True
    b. False

8. After the first big boom in Mustang sales in its first few years of life, Ford witnessed another wave of Mustang fever. What year came in fourth for selling the most Mustangs?
    a. 1968
    b. 1974
    c. 1979
    d. 1994

9. How many Mustang pace cars were made for the 1964 Indianapolis 500?
    a. 35
    b. 100
    c. 1
    d. 3

10. What has been Ford's least popular color family for Mustangs?
    a. Black
    b. Blue
    c. Yellow
    d. Metallic

11. What year were 27,000 right-hand drive Mustangs made?
    a. 1994
    b. 2004
    c. 2005
    d. 2015

12. Prior to the pandemic, what year did the Mustang fare the worst in sales?
    a. 2016
    b. 2009
    c. 1991
    d. 1964 ½

13. How many Ford plants have produced Mustangs over the years?
    a. Four
    b. Eight
    c. Eleven
    d. Sixty-Five

14. What long-distance speed record did the Mustang set in 2020?
    a. Solo Cannonball Run
    b. Cannonball Run
    c. Texas Mile
    d. Parade Run

15. What is Ford's most fuel-efficient Mustang?
    a. 1976 2.3L 4 Cylinder
    b. 1978 King Cobra
    c. 2019 EcoBoost
    d. 2020 Mach-E

16. In 2018, a record was set by one man and his Mustang on which famous track?
    a. Sonoma Raceway
    b. The Nurburgring
    c. Laguna Seca
    d. Circuit de Monaco

17. What car helped Ford win the Sports Car Club of Americas' Championships in 1969 and 1970?
    a. 1968 GT500KR
    b. 1969 Boss 429
    c. 1969 Shelby GT350
    d. 1970 Mach 1

18. Which Shelby Mustang was the first to win a race?
    a. 1967 Mark IV
    b. 1967 GT500
    c. 1965 GT350R
    d. 1964 GT40

19. Possibly the most popular Mustang color in its collective years, how many factory shades of red have Ford offered for the pony model?

    a. 44
    b. 33
    c. 12
    d. Over 50

20. How many times has the Mustang appeared on a U.S. postal stamp?

    a. Twice
    b. Three Times
    c. Five Times
    d. Never

CHAPTER 3 FAST FACTS

- **Most Expensive**

  The most expensive Mustang was auctioned to an anonymous buyer in July 2020 for a record $3.85 million (with taxes and fees). The *Flying Mustang* 1965 Shelby GT350R was built for competition and is one of only two prototypes built. The original *Bullitt* car comes in as the second most expensive Mustang, selling at auction in January 2020 for $3.4 million ($3.7 million after all costs were calculated), although bidding started at a meager $3,500. The Kiernan family had owned the vehicle for over 40 years despite Steve McQueen's attempts to buy the car back over the years. Other record setters include Carroll Shelby's 1967 Shelby GT500 Super Snake which sold for $2.2 million in 2019, the hero car driven by Nicholas Cage which sold for $1 million in 2013, and the first 2020 production Shelby GT500 auctioned for a cool $1.1 million (and the money was donated to charity). It is worth mentioning that the famous Green Hornet was also valued at $3 million in 2012 but didn't meet the $1.8 million reserve while at auction and is still under ownership by the auction house's CEO.

- **Best Selling Years**

  The Mustang's top three bestselling years were in its first three years of production: Ford sold 607,568 Mustangs in 1966, 559,451 in 1965, and 472,121 in 1967. Without a doubt, Ford's First-Generation Mustangs sold more than any subsequent generation, selling 2,981,259 Mustangs by 1973. And with the exception of the cars sold between April and September of 1964, every year of the 60s makes it into the

Mustang's top ten for sales. With the advance of the Fox body and Mustang's Third-Generation, 2,608,812 pony cars were sold—over 14% of them in the first year of that generation, 1979.

- **World's Best Selling Sports Car**
  In 2019, the Mustang earned the title of the best-selling sports car in the world having sold 102,090 cars globally, according to data from IHS Markit. That same year, Mustang yet again came in as the best-selling sports coupe in the world, for the fifth year in a row. Riding high in the global market, the pony car performed well in the United States too. Despite the global pandemic in 2020, they were able to sell 61,090 Mustangs. Ford has ranked as the best-selling sports car in the country for six consecutive years and overall going back 50 years in America's sports car market.

- **Horsepower**
  Ford's 2020 Shelby GT500 Mustang wields an awesome 760 horses and 625 pound-feet of torque—its supercharged Signature Edition offers an additional 40 horsepower—and ranks as the most powerful road-legal vehicle to date that has come out of the Blue Oval's factories. While the dual-clutch transmission is not a new concept, its application in high-performance cars is increasingly state-of-the-art. It is much faster than a manual transmission and doesn't lose the momentum needed to quickly get off the line. *Car and Driver* tested

the stock GT500 in late 2019 and noted its 3.6 second zero to 60 acceleration and 11.4 second quarter-mile at 132 mph. This Mustang beats its closest competitors at the higher speeds and leaves adrenaline junkies wanting more.

- **Most Popular Colors**
As of its Sixth-Generation launch, Ford released information on its three top-selling color choices for 2015. They looked at global sales and considered color options for consumers in the United States, Europe, and China. Across the board, red and black were the most popular color options, but looking more closely at the information, the U.S. stands out with black as its best-selling color. This is in sharp contrast to figures from the First-Generation Mustangs, where only 1.5% of the Mustangs sold were black. More current figures show that Americans also prefer a Magnetic Metallic followed by Ruby Red. In Europe, the bold Race Red ranks number one, while Absolute Black and Deep Impact Blue are second and third, respectively. China's favorite color is also the popular Race Red, followed by Oxford White, and then Black. Ford has offered many shades of red in its 50+ years of selling Mustangs and about 21% of total sales—across all generations—are of the red pony cars. Compared to the dozens of colors offered across the First-Generation of Mustangs, global

marketing teams can scale back the color options and still give consumers what they really want.

- **Mustang Clubs**

  Mustang fans have gravitated toward each other since its earliest days, but it's difficult to pinpoint exactly when they first started organizing. One of such National Mustang Club placed a local newspaper ad in March 1976 to encourage participation. Only about 10 people showed up at its first meeting, but that number increased to over 100 by the next month's meeting and over 250 members by August that same year. Their magazine publication, the Mustang Times has been running monthly since August of 1977. Initially, club membership focused on only the First-Generation of Mustangs, from 1964 ½ - 1973, but in 1986 they opened it up to include Mustangs of all shapes and sizes. The Mustang Club of America is recognized today as the "largest organization of Mustang enthusiasts in the World" with tens of thousands of members around the country.

- **The First Rally**

  Three days before Ford's 1964 unveiling of the Mustang at the World's Fair and about 30 miles north of the location, somewhere around 100 new Mustangs waited for journalists to arrive at the Westchester Country Club in Rye, New York. Once they arrived, members of the media—two at a time—climbed into the new Mustangs and embarked on a historic rally. On the first day, they drove 250 miles to Syracuse, where they were hosted overnight, before traveling 500 miles to headquarters in Dearborn, Michigan, the next day. Ford wined and dined them along the way and afterward even gave members of the media rally prizes. This very first rally was Ford's way of giving the media a first-hand experience with the new Mustang and given the flawless road trip, preferential treatment, and the Mustang's immediate success, there's little room to doubt the journalists' response was anything less than favorable.

Two years later, on the other side of the country, the Southern California Dealer Association resulted in over 1,300 1965 and 1966 model Mustangs converging in a massive—and likely the largest of its time—rally between San Diego and Santa Barbara. Forty-seven years later, the same organization promoted another rally that turned out the same numbers and once again hosted what some believe to be the "largest one-day assembly of a single marque-model" vehicle to date.

- **Largest Mustang Parade**
  Across the pond, Mustang lovers set another record in 2019. This time 1,326 Mustangs from around Europe met at Ford's Lommel Proving Ground in Belgium to

participate in the parade. One after another, the Mustangs headed out in a convoy that succeeded to set the world record for the most Mustangs in a single parade. The European procession beat out the previous Guinness World Record held by Ford for the longest Mustang parade, which was for a 960-pony-car train out of Toluca, Mexico.

CHAPTER 3 TRIVIA ANSWERS

1. b – 1966; the 1966 models experienced the most sales than any other production year—this was the same year Ford made their fully loaded one-millionth Mustang.

2. c – $3,500 according to sources at the *Road & Track* where the ad was placed in 1974, Bob Kiernan was the only one who responded to the post. Decades later when Sean Kiernan, Bob's son, went to sell it at auction, he marveled at the "thousands" of people who made an offer on the original *Bullitt* Mustang after bidding started at the same low price.

3. b – 2007 GT500 Convertible; though the average Mustang weighed in at about 3,500 pounds, the curb weight of this fifth-generation Mustang produced between 2007 to 2010 came in at a hefty 4,040 pounds.

4. c – 1979 Coupe; this base model's curb weight, without any options, was 2,515 pounds.

5. c – 1968 *Bullitt;* the movie famous *Bullitt* had to be photographed, laser scanned, and documented before it was registered in the NVHR's elite database. It was the 21st car to be recognized as a historically significant automobile (there are now 28).

6. d – b & c; the Mustang won *Car of the Year* award in 1974 and again 20 years later in 1994. Ford's whole lineup of cars won the distinction in 1964 for their advanced engineering and performance across several models, but since *technically* the first production

Mustangs were 1965 models, *Motor Trend*'s award would have been reserved for the Fairlane, Falcon, and Thunderbird cars.

7. a – True; Ford's Fox-body platform lasted for a lengthy 26 years, beginning production in 1977 (for the 1978 model year sedans) until it was last used in the 2004 Mustang.

8. b – 1974; maybe surprisingly, the first year of the Mustang II, Ford witnessed that same sort of sales rush, clearing 385,993 Mustangs before the end of 1974 and making it the fourth-best ranking year for sales. With its modest Pinto inspired beginnings, the 1974 Mustang II was smaller and more compact than the year before. Gas prices determined which cars sold and the Mustang II hardtop coupe was flying off the showroom floors.

9. a – 35; even though the Ford Galaxie was scheduled to be the event's pace car that year, Ford replaced the car and sent out 35 Mustangs in time for the May event. Afterward, when committee members could historically purchase the pace cars, demand for the Mustang pace cars was so high, that those in power decided to auction them off to dealerships around the country.

10. c – Yellow; due to the long-running unpopularity of this color, the rarer yellow Mustang owners decided to band together. In 2001, the Yellow Mustang Registry (YMR) was formed, and a website was created to keep fellow yellow Mustang lovers connected.

11. d – 2015; the first year of global sales, Ford made 27,000 right-hand drive models and delivered them to be sold in 81 different countries.

12. b – 2009; official records put 2020 sales as the lowest numbers to date. Before then, 2009 was the lowest year on record for sales, selling only 66,623 Mustangs. Even in the half-year of 1964 ½, sales were nearly double that of 2009 due to the recession.

13. a – Four; the only plant still making Mustangs is the Flat Rock Assembly Plant in Michigan. The other three plants included the Dearborn Assembly Plant (D.A.P., also the original home of Mustangs), Edison (or Metuchen) Assembly in New Jersey, and the San Jose Assembly Plant in Milpitas, California.

14. a - Solo Cannonball Run; driving an average of 108 miles per hour, Fred Ashmore traveled 2,800 miles across the continent—by himself—in a rented Mustang GT. He made the incredible journey in just 25 hours and 55 minutes. In order to pull it off, Ashmore removed all the seats and put in three extra tanks holding a combined 130 gallons of gas. He only had to stop for gas one time.

15. c – 2019 EcoBoost; this 2.3L engine with an automatic transmission got 21 mpg in the city and up to 32 mpg on the highway, for a combined 25mpg. Due to changing emission standards and EPA testing, historic mileage records can be unreliable. The Mustang II was designed around fuel efficiency, and yet the numbers reported aren't an accurate reflection of mileage—the EPA has

since changed which numbers to measure and how to measure them making current numbers more precise.

16. b – The Nurburgring; Formula Drift Champion Vaughn Gittin Jr. set a record as the first and only person to drift all 12.9 miles of the *Green Hell*. Gittin partnered with Ford Performance and other sponsors to upgrade his 2018 Ford Mustang RTR and complete the challenge.

17. d – 1970 Mach 1; at least 2 different people approached Ford with the idea to sponsor rally racing, and so in 1969 the *Ford Rally Team* was born. The group actually consisted of five or six teams nationwide, but each of them drove Mach 1s (some were 351 V8s and others had the 428 Cobra Jet engine).

18. c – 1965 GT350R; driven by Ken Miles, the GT350R was the very first Shelby Mustang model developed for racing. Two prototypes were made before production would be approved for an additional 34 to be sold to customers. The Mustang took first place at a Sports Car Club of America (SCCA) sanctioned race where it managed to take flight briefly and earn its nickname, the Flying Mustang.

19. b – 33; according to paint code records found online, 33 unique designators were identified for shades of red between 1964 and 2020. Ford's Bright Red was offered for more Mustang years than any other red, available from 1971 – 1986, 1989, and again in 1991 – 1993.

20. a – Twice; once in 1999 and again in 2013. The first Mustang was on a 33-cent stamp and featured a 1965

Rangoon Red convertible. The latest, a forever stamp, immortalized the 1967 Shelby GT500 as part of a muscle car stamp collection.

Chapter 4

The Mustang Over Six Generations

TEST YOUR KNOWLEDGE!

1. What color(s) were the 1965 GT350s painted?
   a. Wimbledon White
   b. Wimbledon White & Guardsman Blue
   c. Rangoon Red & Wimbledon White
   d. Silver Smoke Grey

2. Which advertising agency did Ford partner with to market the Ford Mustang?
   a. J. Walter Thomspon
   b. Sid Olsen Ad Agency
   c. Wunderman Thompson
   d. J. Wunderman

3. The 1965 Deluxe Interior Package included what option?

   a. Woodgrain Trim

   b. Pony Embossed Seats

   c. Faux Walnut Steering Wheel

   d. All of the above

4. What year was the fastback replaced with the sportsroof?

   a. 1966

   b. 1967

   c. 1968

   d. 1969

5. The first Mustangs were produced at which Ford plant?

   a. San Jose, CA

   b. Metuchen, NJ

   c. Dearborn, MI

   d. Ionia, MI

6. Fourth Generation Mustangs were the sole Ford model produced on the Fox platform.

   a. True

   b. False

7. In 2008, the Mustang's seats were made with what unique material?
   a. Suede
   b. Hemp Fiber
   c. Lear Foam
   d. Soy Beans

8. What did the Fox-4 refer to?
   a. 3rd Generation Fox body
   b. SN-95 Platform
   c. 5.0 Mustangs
   d. Ford D2C Platform

9. What was the only Mustang prior to the Sixth Generation vehicles to have an independent rear suspension?
   a. 1984 Mustang SVO
   b. 1993 Cobra R
   c. 1999 SVT Cobra
   d. 2001 Bullitt

10. In 1988, Carroll Shelby sued Ford Motor Company for using the GT350 name for its 20th Anniversary Mustang.
    a. True
    b. False

11. Which is not a Sixth Generation Mustang color offered by Ford?

    a. Need for Green
    b. Orange Fury
    c. Magnetic Blue
    d. Royal Crimson

12. Shelby America made the first Shelby Mustang GT350s by converting 1966 notchbacks.

    a. True
    b. False

13. What was the name of the look for the front-end style given to the first several years of the Third Generation Mustangs?

    a. Specs
    b. Block Face
    c. Smooth Nose
    d. Four Eyes

14. What other Ford Motor Company pony car was produced in the US between 1979 and 1986, stealing cues from the Mustang?

    a. Mercury Bobcat
    b. Ford Pinto
    c. Mercury Capri
    d. Cougar XR7

15. Iacocca was given a car in his namesake for Mustang's 45ᵗʰ anniversary.
    a. True
    b. False

16. What years offered the *King of the Road* Mustang?
    a. 1965 and 2005
    b. 1965 and 2015
    c. 1968 and 1998
    d. 1968 and 2008

17. Less than 1,000 Shelby Mustangs were produced in 1970.
    a. True
    b. False

18. When did Ford Mustang go global?
    a. 1965
    b. 1974
    c. 1994
    d. 2015

19. Which Fifth Generation Mustangs were produced without VIN numbers?
    a. S197 II
    b. Shelby *King of the Road*
    c. Cobra Jet
    d. GT California Special

20. What adjective was used by Ford's Senior VP of Design, J Mays, to describe the Fifth-Generation Mustang?
   a. Retro-Futurism
   b. Classically-Crisp
   c. Modern-Vintage
   d. New Edge

CHAPTER 4 FAST FACTS

- **First Generation 1965 – 1973**

  After its non-traditional roll out in 1964, the First-Generation models in 1965 offered a little more variety. The Fastback became an option and buyers could opt for either bucket or bench seats in the convertible and hardtop body styles. Additional options in 1965 included the Deluxe Interior Package and GT Equipment Group. By the end of its first year on the market, the Mustang had surpassed original sales forecasts several times over, selling more than 400,000 cars and outpacing any other Ford models since the Model A almost four decades before. While the fastback would see success in later years, it was significantly less popular in its first year off the line than the hardtop. Additional models and upgrades made widely available for the First-Generation Mustangs included the Shelby Mustangs (GT350 and GT500), Boss 302/351/429, Grande, Mustang GT, and the Mach I.

- **Shelby Mustangs**

  From the first 1966 Shelby GT350s to the increasingly powerful Shelby Mustangs rolling out in recent years, Carroll Shelby's impact on the pony car has not disappointed car lovers. This mainstream race car was not only within reach of Americans, but its performance on the road—proven across American racing circuits against Stingrays, Ferraris, Jaguars, and more—made The Ford Division's *Total Performance* marketing program proud. Ford attached the Cobra moniker to the 1968 GT350 and GT500 models and sold them as Shelby Cobras. That same year, a 428 engine (Cobra Jet) was installed in the GT500 and given the name *King of the Road* as Ford made 1,200 Shelby GT500 KRs. After quality and financial issues caused the California operations of Shelby American Inc. (SAI) to shut down, Shelby Mustangs were freighted to A.O. Smith in Ionia, Michigan, where they were tasked with fixing any issues. During the last couple of years of production, Ford made all the Shelby Mustangs in-house until the contract with Carroll Shelby was terminated in 1969. Production of Shelbys would pick up again in 2005 and continue to this day.

- **Second Generation 1974 – 1978**
  High gas prices weighed heavily on this generation, and Americans demanded cars that were more fuel-efficient. Ford teams made the car smaller (but heavier, with additional equipment required to comply with new emission laws) which in turn, reduced performance. Described as a *gutless wonder*, Second-Generation Mustangs had a desirable front-end suspension, but some might argue that was about the only thing worth value in this generation. Later, Mustang enthusiasts could buy a Mustang II for a low price and put a high-

performance V8 in it, and the body would handle the extra weight without a problem. But in its time, the Mustang II was among the least popular iterations. Buyers could choose between a Hardtop, Hatchback, Mach 1, and Ghia. Small changes over the next couple of years gave consumers the MPG and Stallion options, and the Cobra II and King Cobra in 1976 and 1978, respectively.

- **Third Generation 1979 – 1993**
  Ford's first Fox platform took a late seventies model Cortina and modified its struts to give it a longer wheelbase, bigger trunk, and wider engine bay. By the time this prototype reached production in 1977, it was a 1978 model Fairmont. The platform was in continued use for 26 years across 15 distinct Ford models. Mustang's third-generation cars were the first to be blessed with the Fox body. It was longer and taller than its Second-Generation predecessors, and also offered in coupe, hatchback, or—for the first time in nine years— a convertible body style. A new *Blue Oval* Ford emblem was positioned in the front grille for the first time ever, and the overall front-end styles differed in the first half of this generation compared to the second half. Models and trims continued to be numerous, but a new Turbo GT, SVO, and Cobra R brought changes to the line-up. Additionally, the GT350 in 1984 was recognized as the 20th Anniversary Edition offered in Oxford White, with a

dark red interior, and red stripes along the side rocker panels.

- **Fourth Generation 1994- 2004**

  In 1994, Ford redesigned its pony car, keeping the Fox-body platform but making significant changes. The wheelbase was lengthened from the standard 100.5 inches for Mustangs to 101.3 inches. This new design, the SN-95, ran for the next decade before Ford moved away from the Fox platform entirely. This time, Mustang brought back convertibles and fastbacks but discontinued the notchback and hatchback styles. When production was up and running, Ford released additional options for the new generation including a GT performance package with a 5.0L pushrod V8 engine (this model would go on to be named *Motor Trend's* Car of the Year), Windsor, and Romeo engine options in 1966. It also released a Cobra developed by Ford's Special Vehicle Team (SVT) offered in 1999, 2001, and 2003 – 2004, a purely cosmetic "35th Anniversary Limited Edition" option, a *Spring Feature Edition* for GT models, the Special Edition Bullitt in 2001, and the Mach 1 in 2003 and 2005. A couple more anniversary edition Mustangs were produced—marking Ford's 40th celebration of the Mustang in 2004 and a Centennial Package for Ford Motor Company's 100th Anniversary. Both packages were cosmetic upgrades that reached nearly $1,000.

- **Fifth Generation 2005 – 2014**

  First unveiled as a concept car codenamed *S-197* in 2003, Ford designers were inspired to style the new generation after the very first Mustangs. The Fifth Generation marked a full departure from the Fox-body platform, with the advent of the Ford D2C platform (D-class 2-door coupe). This generation also witnessed the second round of Shelby Mustangs. The very first Shelbys on the market, the CS6 and CS8, were only available as an after-market kit. Ford partnered with Carroll Shelby once again to offer several Shelby models including the Shelby GT/GT-H and bring back the Shelby GT500 and a GT500KR. Over the decade, the pony car saw many model changes: the GT/California Special, Bullitt Mustangs, two 45th Anniversary Edition Mustangs (the 2009 GT and 2009 ½ GT), an S197 II update, 2012 Cobra Jet, and Boss 302. Other options included the Pony Package, the V6 Appearance Package, the V6 Performance Package, Sport Mode, 3.73 Axle Package, Track Package, SVT Performance Package, and many more performance-enhancing upgrades that make the possibilities too many to detail.

- **Sixth Generation**

  In their latest generation of Mustangs, Ford introduced its new S550 platform. The biggest change was Ford's decision to move away from their long-used live axle and go with an independent rear suspension, which many would agree is more balanced and therefore better for real-world driving. Ford would take styling cues from the late 60s Mustang with the *shark-bit* front end and offer a limited number of 50th Anniversary editions in 2015, rocking either of the classic colors, Wimbledon White or Kona Blue. They continue to offer a variety of performance packages from previous years and constantly roll out new special editions. To satisfy the more fuel-conscious consumers, Ford presented the 2.3L EcoBoost engine, turbo-charged with four cylinders of direct injection. To date, several of the latest generations have been recognized by *Car and Driver*, making the *10 Best* list twice and the G.O.A.T. (Greatest of All Time) list in 2020 with the 350 Shelbys.

CHAPTER 4 TRIVIA ANSWERS

1. b – Wimbledon White & Guardsman Blue; All GT350s in 1965 were painted in the Wimbledon White the Guardsman Blue rocker stripes. Somewhere between 150 to 160 of the cars arrived at dealerships with *Le Mans* stripes, which ran the entire length of the car.

2. a - J. Walter Thompson; Ford Motor Company had a long-standing partnership with the J. Walter Thompson advertising agency and remains one of its *oldest* clients (it is now Wunderman Thompson). Employed by JWT as the Copy group head, Sid Olson managed the Mustang account and helped launch the Mustang to stardom.

3. d – All of the above; The Deluxe package was also known as the Pony Interior, Luxury option, and Interior Décor Group, and was available to purchase after the first anniversary of the Mustang.

4. d – 1969; produced in 1968, fastbacks were sold as sportsroof for the 1969 models—they were 4 inches longer, an inch and a half shorter, and offered a more economical engine.

5. c – Dearborn, MI; all of the planning, design, development, and production happened in Dearborn Assembly Plant. The first four generations—over six million—were continuously built in Ford's and even after production was shared with other plants, the Dearborn location has churned out more Mustangs than any of Ford's other locations.

6. a – True; the Mustang was the last Ford model to use the Fox platform. Once the Lincoln Mark VII model was discontinued in 1993, the Fox-body platform would be redefined and kept with the Mustang until Ford stopped using it altogether in 2005.

7. d – Soy Beans; according to Ford's records, Henry Ford approved the use of soy in the Model T where at least 60 pounds of soybeans were present in the paint and plastic parts. One other vehicle—the Model U concept—had soy materials woven into the designs before the announcement of soy-based foam in the 2008 Mustang's seats.

8. b – SN-95 Platform; the Fox body was upgraded for the Fourth-Generation models, and enough changes were made that Ford gave the body family a new code name.

9. c – 1999 SVR Cobra; all first through fifth-generation Mustangs use a solid rear axle, with the single exception of the SVT Cobras produced between 1999 and 2004. 2015 Sixth Generation Mustangs moved to an independent rear suspension.

10. a – True; the GT350 was only produced for 35 days, making 5,261 hatchbacks and convertibles available to the public in 1984 for the 20th anniversary of the Mustang. Apparently, Carroll Shelby was working for Chrysler at the time and had not been consulted about the special project. He sued, Ford stopped making them with the trademarked GT350 stripes, and both parties moved forward.

11. c – Magnetic Blue; Magnetic is a color offered between 2014 and 2019, not Magnetic Blue
12. b – False; Shelby Carroll started with 1965 fastbacks and converted them to the GT350s. They were released in January of 1965 with special features including racing pins and mirrors, louvers, and the iconic side stripes.
13. d – Four Eyes; the angled front end with four blocky headlights gave the illusion of spectacles, hence *Four Eyes*.
14. c – Mercury Capri; the pony car looked similar but had its own style and performance parts.
15. a – True; the 2009 GT ½ was presented to Iacocca as #1 out of 45 production models. The color was named Iacocca Silver in his honor, and the car came with Ford warranties even though it was built by an independent company.
16. d – 1968 and 2008; The Shelby GT500KR *King of the Road* was brought back in the Fifth Generation Mustangs as a tribute to the 60s model, but production was very limited. Only 1011 KRs were made in 2008, and Ford decided to produce the 540 horsepower beast with massive torque again in 2009, making even fewer—712 KRs were made in the final year of production.
17. b – False; No GT350s or GT500s were actually produced into 1970—all of the 1970 Shelby Mustangs were in reality of 1969 models. The 789 unsold cars from 1969 were given new vehicle identification numbers, and a few changes were made before they were sold as 1970

models. The whole *re-VINing* process was of course done with FBI approvals (and under their watchful eye).

18. c – 2012 Cobra Jet; this competition model with 430 horsepower was built and sold in 50-unit batches over several years and designed specifically for racing. For that reason, they come with serial numbers instead of vehicle identification numbers and legally cannot be registered to drive on the roads.

19. a – Retro-futurism; Ford design teams stated that the new 2005 models were styled to pay homage to the classic fastbacks of the late 60s. *New Edge* Mustangs described Ford's Fourth-Generation models.

20. d – 2015; The Sixth Generation Mustangs were marketed and sold to global markets as part of its *One Ford* business strategy. The goal was to streamline operations and produce only what the market demanded. Consequently, the new Mustangs were offered as right-hand or left-hand drive models.

Chapter 5

Other Wild Ponies

TEST YOUR KNOWLEDGE!

1. What is the nickname for the Shelby GT coupe that was unveiled in 1967?
   a. California Special
   b. Super Snake
   c. Shelby Cobra
   d. Little Red

2. Which high-performance car was the first Fox-body Mustang to sport a 5-lug pattern?
   a. 1979 2.3L Turbo 4-Cylinder
   b. 1982 5.0 GT
   c. 1984 SVO Mustang
   d. 1993 Cobra

3. What colors were the 50th Anniversary Edition of the Shelby GTS offered in?

   a. Wimbledon White and Guardsman Blue

   b. Black and Performance White

   c. Race Red and Le Mans White

   d. Kona Blue and Le Mans White

4. How long did Ford run their 1968 *Color of the Month* promotion?

   a. One Year

   b. Six Months

   c. Four Months

   d. Four Years

5. What was the Mustang Junior?

   a. Powercar

   b. Ford Promotion

   c. One-time Raffle Prize

   d. All Of The above

6. At the dawn of the Mustang, which design considered for the pony car was ditched by Ford before it even made it out of its clay stage?

   a. Station Wagon

   b. Four-door Sedan

   c. Rear-facing Rear Seat

   d. Mid-engine Sports Car

7. The Mustang has been a pace car in what two major events?
   a. Monaco Grand Prix and Indy 500
   b. Indy 500 and Le Mans
   c. Indy 500 and Daytona 500
   d. Daytona 500 and Monte Carlo Rally

8. What did Ford recall in the nineties that affected the Mustang, causing overheating and sometimes fires?
   a. Parking Brakes
   b. Ignition Switch
   c. Cruise Control
   d. Fuel Tank

9. What award was presented to Henry Ford II at the World's Fair?
   a. *Motor Trend* Car of the Year
   b. Tiffany's Gold Medal Award
   c. Edmunds Car Award
   d. J.D. Power Award

10. What was the nickname for the scandal—and the car— that Ford Motor Company had plans to build in 1989?
    a. Answer
    b. Answer
    c. Mazdastang
    d. Answer

11. The first *Grabber* paint colors were offered in 1969 Mustangs—how many *Grabber* choices were there in that first year?
    a. One
    b. Twenty Six
    c. Six
    d. Four

12. What was the last Mustang project worked on by Carroll Shelby before his tragic death in 2012?
    a. Shelby GT-H (Hertz Special)
    b. Shelby GT 500 Super Snake
    c. Shelby CS6
    d. 45th Anniversary Edition Shelby GT500

13. Carroll Shelby partnered with which car rental company three times over the course of 50 years to offer a unique Mustang?
    a. Enterprise
    b. Avis
    c. Hertz
    d. National Car Rental

14. What famous building was the Mustang put on top of, not once but twice?
    a. Chrysler Building
    b. Detroit Institute of Art
    c. Trump Tower
    d. Empire State Building

15. Which custom Mustang in 2008 was signed by several actors, a former NASCAR driver and entrepreneur, a Ford executive, an astronaut, and a famous USAF pilot?
    a. AV-X10
    b. AV8R
    c. SR-71
    d. Blue Angels Edition

16. How many Shelby GT350 convertibles were made?
    a. Four
    b. Zero
    c. Fifty
    d. One

17. What Ford model was initially proposed as the vehicle to replace the Mustang in the 1990s?
    a. Pinto
    b. Mazda
    c. Probe
    d. Taurus

18. Which First-Generation territory special had a snake on wheels decal on the Mustang's rear panel?
    a. Sidewinder Special
    b. 429 Cobra Jet
    c. GT350 Cobra
    d. GT500 Cobra

19. A 1968 special out of Oregon offered a distinct golden plaque with the original owner's name engraved in it. What was the name of this special?
    a. Great Golden Gatsby
    b. Gold Ticket Special
    c. Golden Nugget Special
    d. Sunlit Gold Giveaway

20. Ford has never produced a four-door Mustang.
    a. True
    b. False

CHAPTER 5 FAST FACTS

- **The Sprint 200**

  In order to meet the demand for Mustangs and simultaneously off-load less popular Mustang models, Ford introduced the *Springtime Sprint*. The in-line 6-cylinder Mustang was not performing in sales as well as other models, so teams at Ford threw on some painted stripes, a special decal, and a chrome air cleaner and sold the *new* model as a limited-edition Sprint 200. It was mostly marketed to women with the *Six and the Single Girl* catchphrase and came in all three body styles and either automatic or standard transmission.

- **Shelby Hertz**

  In 1966, approximately 1,000 of the Shelby GT350s were converted to GT350H models and resold to the public—and technically, all of them were used cars. Refurbished by Ford, the cars were given a new life. Most were repainted with Hertz colors, but only 85 were given four-speed manual transmission. According to Hertz, all the cars were advertised through their *Rent-a-Racer* Program and could be rented (if the person was over 25) for a cool $17 per day and 17 cents per mile. Naturally, drivers experimented with the 306 horsepower Mustang on the track, causing Hertz's repair costs to become too great to continue the program. When the program came back two more times: in 2006 when Hertz offered the Shelby GT-H Mustangs through their "Fun Collection" and again in 2016 as part of the "Adrenaline Collection" recognizing the 50th anniversary of their collaboration.

- **1966 High Country Special**
  This lesser-known special edition was marketed primarily to the Rocky Mountain states and are exceptionally rare. The High Country Mustangs came in Columbine Blue, Aspen Blue, and Timberline Green, which were all factory-offered colors at the time, but sported a unique badge with the Mustang running above a mountain skyline. They were all produced at Ford's San Jose plant and shipped to dealers around Colorado. By 1968, the HCS was only available as a hardtop. No more than 1,000 HCS Mustangs were made in the three years they were in production, and Ford moved on with the California Special.

- **The Tussy Cosmetic Sweepstakes**
  One of the many early promotions to drum up interest for the Ford Mustang, a full-page advertisement for Tussy's new line of pink lipstick shades offered wearers Racy Pink, Racy Pink Frosted, and Defroster. When buying their favorite shade of lipstick, fans could enter the sweepstakes, win a 1967 convertible and "Wear a Mustang to match your lipstick!" According to the ad,

only "five lucky winners" got their hands on one of these custom-colored Mustangs.

- **1967 Shelby Mustangs**
  When Ford wanted to go bigger, a few big-block Shelby GT cars were proposed with a 7.0L V8 engine: the first GT500, a single Shelby GT coupe, and a Shelby GT500 convertible. These race-track-worthy Shelby Mustangs tested as the fastest production car in its time to ever take a lap at Ford's test loop (this didn't include their top racer, the GT40). A lone fastback was upgraded with the Ford GT40's powerful 427 FE engine and nicknamed the *Super Snake*. As a promotion with Goodyear, Shelby demonstrated the awesomeness of this performance car by running it on a track for 500 miles, clocking an average speed of 142 mph. The Goodyear Thunderbolt tires held up, the GT500's reputation soared, and Shelby hoped to make more. Unfortunately, the project never got off the ground, putting the single 1967 Super Snake among the rarest of cars.

- **The Green Hornet**
  This Mustang was rescued by Fred Goodell of Shelby American from Ford's prototype collection for the California Special Mustang. What started as a 1968 GT500, the Green Hornet went through some serious upgrades under Shelby and Goodell's supervision: a new 428 Cobra Jet V8, Conelec electronic fuel-injection system,

six-speed automatic transmission, independent rear suspension, improved front suspension, and rear disc brakes. The dark metallic green paint job and black hardtop gave it its nickname (supposedly by Bill Cosby), and despite its impressive performance, the car was turned away as a production design. The single Green Hornet was sold several times before landing at Barret Jackson auction-house under the ownership of CEO Craig Jackson.

- **California Special aka GT/CS**
  Another Shelby GT500 prototype, the GT/CS in its earliest form, was influenced by Carroll Shelby and Chief Engineer Fred Goodell after producing their favorite little coupe, *Little Red*. The first models were coupe bodies with a choice of engines and transmissions. From the smallest 289 to the 428 Cobra Jet V8, Mustang buyers could pick any powertrain alongside a manual or automatic transmission. Just a few of the unique exterior features included a custom hood to accommodate the engine possibilities, special badges, paint, and three-wheel choices, in addition to a number of cosmetic interior upgrades. The earliest California Specials were sent to 4,100 dealerships around California in 1968 and wouldn't be offered again for 40 years. In 2007, Ford brought back the GT/CS as an exterior package upgrade and made it available to buyers in every state.

- **1971 Shelby Europa**

  Made in 1970, only nine 1971 *Shelby Europas* were produced in Europe under a special license with Belgian dealer Claude Dubois. Six were GT350 Sportsroofs, one was a GT500 Sportsroof, and two were GT500 convertibles. This was the only Mustang to be marketed in Europe before Ford released the Sixth-Generation Mustangs.

- **McLaren Mustang of 1980**

  As a result of Ford Motor's partnership with McLaren Performance, the McLaren Mustang was born. Ford planned to make 249 cars in order to demonstrate the compatibility and performance of the Mustang with a proven name in racing, the McLaren. However, only ten of these 1980 Fox-body cobras with turbocharged four-cylinders and 131 horsepower were ever made. Ford went on to create their own internal team, the Special Vehicle Operations department and terminated their relationship with McLaren. At least one existing and functional McLaren Mustang still exists, and with the reported less-than 524 miles on the odometer, its value is no doubt high.

- **The Mustang SVO**

  For the decade before Ford's Special Vehicle Team (SVT) was created, the team operated as the Special Vehicle

Operations (SVO) department. In their entire existence, the only production car to come out of SVO's portfolio was the Ford Mustang SVO, selling about 9,835 of the Fox-body models between 1984 and 1986. The sporty car offered a 2.3L, turbocharged four-cylinder engine with up to 205 horsepower—enough to compete with Ford's V8 5.0L engine. Because of its light frame, electronic fuel injection with an intercooler, and a strategically placed engine (just behind the front axle), the SVO beat the GT's zero to 60MPH time by about 1.3 seconds. Modifications varied in the few years it was offered, but a T-5 transmission, Hurst shifter, 16" wheels, front and rear disc brakes, and a 5-lug pattern were among the performance equipment that remained the same. Ford's team also had the bright idea to put a brake pedal from an automatic transmission as the clutch pedal in order to improve the driver's shifting ability.

- **Ford Mustang SSP:**
  This Special Service Package (SSP) vehicle came out while Ford was using the Fox-body platform and a 5.0L engine, providing law enforcement agencies around the country with the speed needed to step up their game in high-speed pursuits. Additional options to beef up the patrol cars included a certified and calibrated speedometer, coolers, and silicone hoses to keep the engine oil and auto transmission fluid temperatures

down. Other options include a heavy-duty alternator, safety lights, and reinforced floors to make a stiffer chassis for maneuvering at high speeds. It was the California Highway Patrol (CHP) that went to Ford and asked them for a better solution to the heavy body cruisers they were running. When Ford came up with the SSP in 1982, the CHP ordered 400 immediately. Nearly 15,000 more were made and sent to over thirty states including Canada, and California would buy up its share. Heralded as a long-time favorite of the *Chippies*, the Mustang still had a major drawback: its small size. Limited interior space (with all the additional required equipment law enforcement needed) and only 2 doors made arresting and transporting criminals nearly impossible. Some CHP would get creative and *secure* the handcuffs via a nylon strap to the back floorboards, keeping perpetrators restrained. Long term, the more powerful V8 engines and bigger bodies of the Camaros, Caprices, and Dodge Chargers met the needs in ways that the 2,500 Mustangs used across the California Highway Patrols couldn't.

- **The Bullitt Mustangs**
  Revived in 2001, the Bullitt GT combined performance with some of the original fastback styling cues to provide buyers a clean, classic sports car. It offered better intake and exhaust, giving it just enough extra horsepower and torque to deliver more power off the

line. Ford's track testing showed that the Bullitt GT beat the standard GT with faster 0–60 and quarter-mile times (5.8 seconds and 14.3 seconds compared to 6.0 and 14.7). Between the performance upgrades and the better brakes, improved suspension package, and lower frame, the heritage car's over-responsive and stable handling makes it stand out from the crowd. Ford brought the Bullitt car back as an option for 2008/2009 models and again a decade later for the 2019/2020 lineup on the s550.

- **Military Aviation Mustangs**
  For over a decade, Ford has been raising money for charity with its one-of-a-kind Mustangs modeled after aviation greats. Each equally impressive themed vehicle was sold at auction to benefit the Young Eagles and hopeful future aviators of the Experimental Aircraft Association (EEA). To date, the charity auction has raised over $3 million. The custom models include (in chronological order, from 2008 to 2019) the Mustang AV8R, the AV-X10 Dearborn Doll, SR-71 Blackbird Edition, GT Blue Angels Edition, Tuskegee Airmen Red Tails Edition, U.S. Air Force Thunderbirds Edition, Lockheed Martin F-35 Lightning II, Apollo Edition, Bob Hoover P-51 Ole Yeller GT350 Shelby, F-22 Raptor F-150 Raptor, Eagle Squadron Mustang GT, and the Old Crow Mustang GT.

- **Boss 302 Laguna Seca Edition**
The 2012 Boss 302 came back with a limited production of Laguna Seca edition offered for two years. Buyers could choose between Black or Ingot silver, both with red accents, in 2012, and School Bus Yellow or Black, with silver accents. Only about 1500 of these Boss Mustangs were made in total over the two years and were designed to perform on a track. Among the unique final touches is a rear badge featured with an outlined map of the famous Laguna Seca track and Ford's TrackKey—a special key that, when driven with it in the ignition, allows the amateur racer to harness all 444 horses for maximum performance.

- **Hoonicorn**
This drifting extraordinaire was gifted to the world by Ken Block and Hoonigan Racing Division, plus automotive heroes Jack Roush, Vaugh Gittin and his team at RTR Vehicles, and a slew of industry experts offering their latest and greatest performance parts. The 1965 notchback was completely overhauled and transformed to include a high-end 6-speed transmission and a custom-built turbocharged 410 cubic inch V8 channeling 845 horsepower and 720 pound-feet of torque. Ken's team went on to introduce a second version, the Hoonicorn RTR, by modifying the first Hoonicorn to increase its horsepower to an incredible 1,400 ponies and 1,250 ft-lb of torque and giving it a 2.7

second 0–60 and a top speed of an incredible 211 miles per hour. Hoonigan's team has revealed another Mustang project in the works: the Hoonifox, an AWD 1965 Fox body, sure to impress anyone who bears witness.

CHAPTER 5 TRIVIA ANSWERS

1. d – Little Red; in 1967, the serial number ending in 0131 was the only Shelby GT coupe built. It started as a notchback coupe and was upgraded to a GT500. The original Candyapple Red hardtop was painted over with Ford's Calypso Coral (a nod to the Ferrari Red color at the time) and a black vinyl top. Several engines and transmission combinations were tested out before Shelby Chief Engineer Fred Goodell settled on a first time ever Paxton supercharged 428 engine and a *Shelbyized* 6-cylinder transmission. Other firsts included a power antenna mounted on the trunk, cooling hood louvers, and a custom coupe decklid made from fiberglass.

2. c – 1984 SVO Mustang; the SVO was the first Fox-body Mustang with a 5-lug factory setup (in order to accommodate the bulky factory disc brakes), although 5 lug conversion kits are widely available now.

3. b – Black and Performance White; Shelby American produced only 100 50th Anniversary Edition GTS—50 Black and 50 Performance White.

4. c – Four Months; the nationwide promotion offered a specially priced Mustang in a different color each month to dealerships. While Ford provided the spring-themed paint colors, it is believed that the dealerships could choose the names each month. A gold color was offered in January (New Year's), pink in February (Valentine's

Day), green in March (St. Patrick's Day), and coral in April (Easter). One example from Denver named the color options Black Hills Gold, Passionate Pink, Emerald Green, and Eastertime Coral.

5. d – All Of The above; Ford Motor Company first partnered with the Powercar Company in 1954 to build *junior* versions of its Thunderbird for marketing purposes. By 1964, Ford had them making Mustang Juniors in order to deliver to dealerships and bring in more customers. They even went so far as to bring the mini-cars into schools and hand out *tickets* for the kids to bring their parents in to see the full-sized beauties on the showroom floor. Ford had about 600 made, either gas-powered or electric, raffling off some and selling the rest to promote the Mustang.

6. a – Station Wagon; this build was made out of clay in Ford's design studios and never went farther than that inside Ford's walls. However, *outside of Ford*, a small team of motivated car guys sent a 1965 289 hardtop Mustang to Construzione Automobili Intermeccanica to be converted into a Mustang. In the meantime, Ford had moved on to other models, but the rare station wagon was sent back to the states where it has been lost to time.

7. c – Indy 500 and Daytona 500; There were only 4 occasions in which the Mustang participated in NASCAR's events as a pace car—three times in the Indy

500 (1964, 1979, and 1994) and once in the Daytona 500, in 2011.

8. b – Ignition Switch; considered its second-biggest recall—Ford's first, their powertrain recall, which was also the largest recall for any single car manufacturer—Ford recalled just under 8 million vehicles and had to replace the ignition switches across its brand, which included the late eighties and early nineties model Mustangs.

9. b – Tiffany's Gold Medal Award; though later it was revealed to have been a promotional deal worked out between the two companies. Ford received the award from the diamond company at the 1964 New York World's Fair. The award recognized the Mustang for "Excellence in American Design," and was celebrated with key chain medallions made by Ford.

10. a – Mazdastang; when Ford was recovering from their ignition switch recall, they were considering moving the Mustang to a front-wheel-drive platform. Donald Farr, the editor of Mustang Monthly, used his platform to gain traction for the resistance, providing readers with then Ford President's address headquarters to forward their complaints. In the end, Ford scrapped the plan, Mazdastang was averted, and Mustang lovers heaved a collected sigh of relief.

11. d – Four; The first colors offered with the Grabber theme were Grabber Blue, Grabber Green, Grabber Yellow, and Grabber Orange, only on the Shelby

Mustangs. The next year, all four colors were available in standard Mustang models. Grabber Lime and Light Grabber Blue were added next in 1971 and 1974, respectively. Hues changed slightly over the years, and some colors were offered in years where others weren't, but the Grabber paint choices have been options in a total of sixteen production years in the Mustang's lifetime to date.

12. b - Shelby GT500 Super Snake; the 2011 Mustang was in fact, the very last specialty car Shelby ever worked on. He collaborated with Electronic Arts from the Need for Speed video game franchise to make the one-of-a-kind car in order to raise money for the Carroll Shelby Foundation. According to Barrett Jackson's auction site, it sold for $79,200 in 2017.

13. c – Hertz; Shelby and Hertz worked together in 1966 for the GT350H and again in 2006 & 2016 to offer the GT-H. They always marketed with Hertz's corporate colors. The black and Le Mans gold racers are fairly rare (only an estimated 2,000 – 2,200 cars were part of the original programs) and therefore considered to be collectors in the classic car world.

14. d - Empire State Building; in October of 1965, a white Mustang was quartered and in 6 hours overnight hoisted up the 86 floors of the famous New York building and reassembled on the observation deck. It was removed inside the glass area on the 86th floor after it posed for photos and stayed there on display for

five months. The stunt was repeated for the Mustang's 50th birthday, this time with a yellow Mustang no one would miss it.

15. b – AV8R; the first in a series of aviation-themed custom Mustangs. The AV8R was signed by Edsel B Ford II, USAF pilot Chuck Yeager, astronaut Jim Lovell, actors Harrison Ford, John Travolta, Morgan Freeman, and the well-known Jack Roush.

16. a – Four; Carroll Shelby secretly worked on the four convertibles in 1966, making only four of them for his friends and family. Each Shelby convertible was painted a different color.

17. c – Probe; intended as the newest iteration of Mustangs to represent its Fourth Generation, the Probe was a smaller coupe—a sport compact to be precise. The front-wheel-drive was a huge problem for Mustang purists, coupled with the underwhelming engine options and foreign parts. So with enough pushback, Ford was convinced to go in a different direction for the Fourth-Generation Mustangs. Instead, their front-wheel drive plans produced the Probe.

18. a – Sidewinder Special; in 1970, Ford made 40 special edition Mustangs that went beyond the aesthetic-only packages. These rare and distinctive vehicles were built with a 351 V4 engine and the increasingly popular Cruise-O-Matic.

19. c – Golden Nugget Special; Ford scheduled 525 Limited Edition Mustangs in Sunlit Gold (color code Y) to be built

with a black vinyl top, louvered hood, a black interior, and the owner engraved gold dashboard plaque. In reality, only 481 Golden Nugget Mustangs came to be.

20. b – False; at the time of this publication, the 2021 Mustang Mach-E with four doors can be ordered from Ford's website. As a five-passenger SUV, the Mustang offers more interior space than any of its predecessors. This is also the first official electric vehicle to be produced on any significant scale.

Chapter 6

The Mustang in Hollywood

TEST YOUR KNOWLEDGE!

1. What famous Hollywood production was the first major motion picture to feature Ford's new Mustang?
   a. *Goldfinger*
   b. *Gone in 60 Seconds (1974 Version)*
   c. *From Russia With Love*
   d. *Dr. No*

2. According to official records, *Goldfinger* movie producers kept the original white convertible Mustang used in filming and later used it in what other movies?
   a. *Thunderball*
   b. *You Only Live Twice*
   c. *Diamonds Are Forever*
   d. It was not used in any other movies

3. What colors were Sonny & Cher's 1966 coordinating custom convertibles?
   a. CandyApple Red and Champagne Beige
   b. Racy Pink and Defroster
   c. Hot Candy Pink and Murano Gold
   d. Playmate Pink and Sauterne Gold

4. What model car is *Eleanor*?
   a. Shelby GT500
   b. 1971 Sportsroof
   c. Customized 1973 Fastback
   d. All of the above

5. Which Mustang appeared in Steve McQueen's 1968 *Bullitt*?
   a. 1968 Mustang Bullitt
   b. 1968 GT Fastback
   c. 1967 Shelby GT500
   d. 1966 Shelby GT350H

6. In what movie was the Mustang featured as the first car where filming took place inside the vehicle?
   a. *Goldfinger*
   b. *Gone in 60 Seconds (1974)*
   c. Steve McQueen's *Bullitt*
   d. *Starman*

7. How many versions of Steve McQueen's famous Bullitt Mustang has Ford relaunched over the years?
   a. One
   b. Two
   c. Three
   d. Five

8. Toby Halicki's widow is the only one legally allowed to make (or approve) any reproduction *Eleanor* Mustangs.
   a. True
   b. False

9. Which Mustang makes an appearance as Jeff Bridge's alien-playing-human clone learns to drive in 1984's *Starman*?
   a. 1977 Cobra II
   b. 1980 GT Hatchback
   c. 1983 Fox-body Coupe GT
   d. 1984 SVO

10. What Mustang edition was brought back to the screen in the 2000 remake of *Gone in Sixty Seconds*?
    a. Super Snake
    b. Shelby GT500
    c. Ford GT40
    d. GT Fastback

11. What other popular movie in 2003 featured a Saleen S281 Mustang?
    a. *xXx: State of the Union*
    b. *Fun with Dick and Jane*
    c. *Bruce Almighty*
    d. *2 Fast 2 Furious*

12. What Tom Cruise movie in 2005 featured him driving a 1966 Shelby GT350H?
    a. *The Last Samurai*
    b. *Mission Impossible III*
    c. *War of the Worlds*
    d. *Collateral*

13. In the sci-fi saga, *Transformers,* which Decepticon was disguised as a Saleen S281 Mustang Police Car?
    a. Barricade
    b. Brawl
    c. Bonecrusher
    d. Blackout

14. What popular Will Smith movie features him driving a bright red Shelby GT500?
    a. *Bad Boys*
    b. *Hitch*
    c. *I Am Legend*
    d. *Pursuit of Happyness*

15. In *Bucket List,* Morgan Freeman crosses off *Drive a Shelby Mustang* after driving a bright red 1966 GT350.
    a. True
    b. False

16. A 1973 Ford Mustang Mach 1 has a starring role in which British Comedy series?
    a. *The Office*
    b. *The IT Crowd*
    c. *Extras*
    d. *Saxondale*

17. What Shelby Mustang did Ethan Hawke and Selena Gomez drive in the 2013 car-wrecking production *Getaway*?
    a. 2007 GT500 SVT
    b. 2007 GT500 Super Snake
    c. 2013 GT500 Super Snake
    d. a & b

18. The 2014 Norwegian action-comedy film series *BØrning* stars car enthusiast Roy and his treasured Lillegul. What kind of Mustang is Lillegul?
    a. 1968 GT 289
    b. 1967 2+2 Fastback 289
    c. 1968 GT Hardtop 302
    d. 1967 Hardtop Coupe 390

19. Keanu Reeves drove a Mustang Mach 1 in two different movies: *John Wick* and ____?
    a. *Point Break*
    b. *Much Ado About Nothing*
    c. *Speed*
    d. *My Own Private Idaho*

20. In 2014's *Need for Speed,* what famous movie with a Mustang is playing on the drive-in movie theater screen?
    a. *Gone in Sixty Seconds* (2000)
    b. *Gone in 60 Seconds* (1974)
    c. *Bullitt*
    d. *Goldfinger*

CHAPTER 6 FAST FACTS

- According to Ford Motor Company, Mustangs have appeared in over 500 movies as well as hundreds of television programs. Further, Bob Witter's statement from Ford Global Brand Entertainment (FGBE) claimed that the "Mustang have had the most roles of any Ford vehicle, and there are no competing cards that come close." The Internet Movie Cars Database (IMCDB) identifies over 4,500 filmed appearances—in TV and movies—where the Mustang makes an appearance, typically in fast-paced, high-action films. And Ford's relationship with Hollywood has certainly proved to be lucrative. The company went on to describe that "filmmakers often use the Mustang as a way to help define a character because there is something about its styling and what the brand means that symbolizes quintessential American cool. If a filmmaker wants a character to look cool, clever, and tough, a great way to convey that is by putting him behind the wheel of a Mustang." Looking back at its starring roles, it is easy to see the reciprocal relationship that has benefited both pop culture and Mustang sales for over 50 years.

- *Goldfinger*, **1964**
  Filming for *Goldfinger* actually began before the Mustang was in commercial production. Hence, the filmmakers tapped British company Alan Mann Racing,

who was plugged into the European rally circuit where Ford had tested its concept cars. And in 1964, movie theater-goers around the U.S. witnessed a white Mustang convertible driven by Tilly Masterson (Tania Mallet) in hot pursuit of James Bond (played by Sean Connery driving his signature Aston Martin) over Switzerland's Furka Pass in the Swiss Alps.

- *Grand Prix,* **1966**
  Featuring European race tracks, actual racing footage, real-life race car drivers, and Formula One World Champions, this movie makes everyone feel like they can be in the races. James Garner, who played American FI driver Pete Aron in the movie, also held part ownership in an auto racing team in the late 1960s. The Mustang doesn't have a starring role in this film, but it just so happens to be the personal vehicle of choice for one of the movie's main protagonists: when not racing, Pete Aron drives a flashy black and gold 1966 Shelby GT350H to up his *cool* factor.

- *Good Times,* **1967**
  Nearly a decade before iconic celebrity couple Sonny and Cher split, the duo made a movie together—with coordinating Mustangs! Even though this movie lost more money than it made, it was reported that the cast had a good time making it after firing an original screenwriter. The musical comedy shows off their highly

customized—and some might say ostentatious—Mustang convertibles. It was reported that Ford wanted to gift the couple Mustangs to help boost sales, but before they handed over the cars, they let George Barris, dubbed the *King of the Kustomizers* and a Hollywood favorite go-to car guy, upgrade the convertibles. In addition to some unique exterior choices (for example, 40 layers of custom paint and the door handles were removed), both convertibles had over the top interiors that included shag carpets, leather and suede seats, state of the art eight-track stereos, and swivel seats for the driver. With serial numbers separated by a single digit, the pair were sold years later at auction to a private collector for $137,000. They are now retired together, on display in Kansas City's Midwest Dream Car Collection.

- **Bullitt, 1968**
  Steve McQueen's action thriller film is the first movie where the audience gets a first-person view from within the car during a chase scene. This may also be why it is still revered as one of the best car chase scenes coming out of Hollywood. Two 1968 four-speed manual Fastbacks with V8 390 cubic inch engines were provided by Ford, likely as a marketing agreement with Warner Brothers. They were modified by a reputable car builder in Hollywood, Max Balchosky, who removed the running horse emblem, GT fog lights from the wheel,

and added American Racing five-spoke wheels and a steering wheel out of a 67 Shelby GT500. As a result of the jumps and hard landings from chase scenes around the San Francisco streets, one of the Highland Green Fastbacks had to be scrapped (though it has since been discovered in Mexico, where it was salvaged and is now being restored). Records show that the other serial number was purchased by an employee of the film studio and sold several times before it ended up with a private party buyer who casually used the car with his family for several decades—despite Hollywood's attempt to bring it back into the spotlight.

- *Diamonds Are Forever,* **1971**
  In Sean Connery's final role as James Bond, secret agent drives a 1971 red Mustang Mach 1. Sources indicate that six Mach 1s were used mostly with 302 two-barrel engines, but the car seen most frequently with the actor ran 429 cubic inch Super Cobra Jet engine sporting a whopping 375 horsepower. This high-powered engine gave it the torque it needed to burn rubber and circle cop cars during the chase scenes. However, the most popular car chase scene in the film is remembered because of its visible goof, which made it past the final edits: the mustang enters a narrow alley on its two right wheels but exits on the two left wheels.
- *Gone in 60 Seconds,* **1974**

In 1974 "Toby" Halicki self-produced the film *Gone in 60 Seconds*. There remains a lot of debate on forums around the internet about whether the yellow Mustangs used in the original *Gone 60 Seconds* movie were 1973 or 1971 models. Several sources close to the project, including Denise Halicki, the widow of H.B. "Toby" Halicki, Lee Iaccoca, and even the website of Fusion Motor Company (who has been authorized to make copyrighted rebuilds by Halicki's widow) have referred to *Eleanor* as a 1973 model. However, Internet research indicates that the cars were purchased in 1971, years before Halicki started filming, and thus would indicate they did, in fact, begin as 1971 models. Halicki wanted the newer 1973 Fastbacks for filming purposes, so he made a number of modifications to make the yellow and black Mustang fall in line with his vision.

- *Charlie's Angels,* TV Series 1976 – 1981
  There were actually at least 10 Ford Mustangs used at different times in the popular 70s television series, but only two had significant screen time. Lead character Kelly Garret drove a yellow 1967 Mustang II and later a 1977 tan Mustang II Ghia with the Sports Group package. Farrah Fawcett's character, Jill Munroe, first drove the white 1967/1977 Second Generation Mustang Cobra II with blue racing stripes, and while the car remained in the series until the final season, Farrah

did not. Both Mustangs have enough screen time to be fixtures alongside their famous actress counterparts, and there are even scenes where the two Mustangs were parked side by side.

- **Bull Durham, 1988**
  Rumor has it that the Highland Green 1968 Shelby GT350, driven by Kevin Costner in the movie, was later purchased by his wife as a gift to him. Apparently, the star really liked the car, so his wife had the movie Mustang restored and given as a present to him.

- **Back to the Future Part II, 1989**
  In this highly anticipated sequel, Doc and Marty did some time traveling and encounter both old and very unusual futuristic models of familiar vehicles. Fans have pointed out two Mustangs in this movie: one, an older, undated coupe, and the other, a highly modified 87 to 89 bright red Mustang GT that definitely looks like something from the future.

- **Basic Instinct, 1991**
  Driving a 1990 Mustang GT Convertible, Michael Douglas shows fans the incredible climbing power of his character's pony car. The Mustang takes a shortcut up an entire flight of stairs in hot pursuit of the high-end Lotus Esprit, making this car chase scene worth watching.

- **Team Knight Rider, TV Series 1997 – 1998**

  The *Knight Rider* spin-off series only lasted one season but offered 22 episodes of crime-fighting action by talking cars. Like Michael Knight's KITT, there are five team vehicles with artificial intelligence (AI) that allows them to talk and interact with their drivers. In the series, each vehicle displays a different and unique personality. The modified red and white 1996 SVT Cobra convertible driven by team member Jenny (actress Christine Steel)—and who may be Michael Knight's daughter—is named Domino or DMO-1, an overly talkative and flirty AI with a woman's voice (played by Nia Vardalos). A 2008 tv series and made for tv movie re-imaged KITT as the vehicle that can transform into several other vehicles, though it maintains a Mustang rear seat in the new series. One of KITT's disguises is a 1969 Mach 1 Mustang.

- **Thomas Crown Affair, 1999**

  In the remake of the film, producers paid homage to the 1968 film with Steve McQueen by putting Pierce Brosnan in highly modified 1968 Shelby Mustang GT500. The car was a one-off, off-road convertible built by true Mustang fan and overall gearhead Gino Lucci and his company Picture Cars East out of Brooklyn, New York. Mr. Lucci was an established name in Hollywood, having built movie cars for over 40 years, and revealed the Mustang's origins. Fans might be interested to learn that the 68 Shelby starring in the film actually started as a small-block 1967 Mustang GTA convertible with various Shelby parts, and it was originally destined for a role in *Last Action Hero* with Arnold Schwarzenegger. It wasn't until the pony car arrived and the film crew realized it was just too small for the action star's large frame that the vehicle was then *shelved*. Director John McTiernan pulled the car out of his Wyoming barn some years later and had it shipped to Gino's company on the east coast, where the crew there had to clean squirrel remains out of the dashboard before they could get started on the work. Lucci and his guys worked off a sketch from McTiernan's vision and made it into the GT500 off-roading beast we see in the movie, complete with a roll bar, raised suspension, chunky tires, and a spare tire hitched to the back. Although the Hollywood car has disappeared from sight, a die-hard fan went to great lengths to have a visual replica built by Classic Design Concepts (CDC) in Detroit, with modern functionality. This Michigan farmer even requested to have the doors welded shut just like in the movie but was talked out of it by the founder of CDC, George Huisman. The Michigander has remained anonymous, but a stunning photo gallery and article detailing his recreation can be fully appreciated on the web.

- **Gone in Sixty Seconds, 2000**
  The 1967 Shelby GT500 *Eleanor* reminded Americans why they loved this car. According to records, up to 12 Mustangs were built to be used for the production of the remake, and they were all different. One prototype wasn't actually used in the movie at all—the only true Shelby GT500, made for the movie's producer, Jerry Bruckheimer—and three were built to be fully functional vehicles. While all of the cars started out with 67 Fastbacks bodies, they were so highly modified and experimented with that by the end of filming, and counting only seven cars that didn't end up scrapped. It's hard to know how exactly each car started. However, it is on record that Nicholas Cage did many of his own car chase scenes (after completing two different driving schools) in a black 1965 Mustang fastback. As a result of the 2000 remake of this film, the Pro Touring and restomod scenes galloped back into popularity, as did *Eleanor* look-alikes.

- **Hollywood Homicide, 2003**
  The limited-edition Mustang silver S281 convertible was custom made by Saleen Automotive, an American automaker pushing out special-edition, mass-produced cars since 1984. After having the car featured in a movie with the likes of Josh Hartnett and Harrison Ford—not to mention a nearly 20-minute car chase scene—Steve Saleen capitalized on the advertising and came up with

a *Hollywood Homicide* edition to sell to eager consumers.

- **The Fast and the Furious: Tokyo Drift, 2006**
  The Fast and the Furious franchise hosted many lust-worthy cars over the years. The Mustang had a few roles across the lengthy series, including *2 Fast 2 Furious* (2003), *Fast & Furious* (2008), and *Fast & Furious 6* (2013), but it saw the most screen time in the 2006 sequel, *Tokyo Drift*. The car in the movie was painted and modified to look somewhat like the distinctive Shelby models. Still, it was actually its own kind of Mustang with a 1967 fastback body, a Nissan 2.6L RB26 inline-six engine (from a Nissan Skyline GT-R), and a 430-inch Windsor motor with a 9-inch rear end and spool, giving it nearly 500 horsepower.

- **Death Race, 2008**
  Made to look like something out of a *Mad Max* movie, the 2006 GT was very heavily modified. In the film, Jason Statham inherits the car from his predecessor, Frankenstein, and drives the part race car, part death machine in a race for survival. Up to six Mustangs were used to film, but not all of them required all the performance and design modifications. Statham's winning war machine was converted to have suicide doors and enough horsepower to carry all the extra

weight of the many on-board weapons and faux (plastic) armor.

- **Need For Speed, 2014**

  Just like in the plot, this 2013 GT is a custom project. As one of Carroll Shelby's unfinished projects, the storyline transforms the Mustang into a one-off GT500. In real life, only one true Shelby GT500 was used as the *hero car*, and the other six cars used for filming were 2014 model GTs donated by Ford for customization. At the very end of the film, the unreleased 2015 Mustang made a brief appearance—something filmmakers worked hard to make happen since the car wasn't officially ready to be unveiled to the public for another six months. It was a high-risk mission to transport the prototype car from Michigan to Nevada without being seen, but with the help of lots of additional security, local police, and Ford's calibration team (who loaned the prototype out for filming), chief engineer Dave Pericak was able to get the Mustang to the film set and back home again without any publicity leaks.

- **John Wick, 2014**

  John Wick's 1969 Ford Mustang Mach 1 is coveted by a Russian gangster at a gas station. That tense moment (when the car is mistakenly described as a Boss 429) sets the tone for what comes next in the movie. Keanu Reeve's character had just lost his wife, and after a violent break-in leaves him without his Mustang and his new puppy, he sets out on a path of destruction to get back what was taken from him—or maybe just exact revenge. Five Mustangs were destroyed for the film production, and John Wick doesn't get his Mustang back until the sequel in 2017.

- *A Faster Horse*, **2015**
  In this Netflix Documentary, viewers get a peek inside Ford facilities and the people, efforts, and secrecy around the Mustang. Key voices over at Ford discuss the latest Mustang and celebrate the 50th anniversary of the pony car while reflecting on its development over so many years. As one man states, "Everybody has a Mustang story. You don't have to own one to have one."

CHAPTER 6 TRIVIA ANSWERS

1. a – *Goldfinger*; Hollywood seized the opportunity to showcase Ford's new pony car, finding a source in Europe to provide them with a new Mustang for the Bond movie.

2. d – It was not used in any other movies; records indicate the car never left Europe after its appearances in *Goldfinger* and its whereabouts to this day are unknown.

3. c – Hot Candy Pink and Murano Gold; maybe not the only Mustangs ever painted in these custom colors but certainly the most famous. Interestingly, the other colors listed are all real color options offered at some time in history.

4. d – All of the above; cars from the original film both started as 1971 Mustang Sportsroof bodies and were modified to look like 1973 Fastbacks. In the 2000 remake, the film team chose a Shelby GT500 to play *Eleanor*.

5. b – 1968 GT Fastback; after a family tragedy and through a series of well-timed coincidences, many non-disclosure agreements, and Ford's 50th-anniversary celebration of its beloved pony car, the Highland Green fastback from the filming of *Bullitt* was rolled out to a largely unsuspecting but equally excited audience. It was the first time in over 40 years that Mustang fans were able to glimpse the long-lost but not forgotten

Bullitt Mustang. It toured around the world for two years before setting a sales record at auction in 2020.

6. c – Steve McQueen's *Bullitt;* the scenes filmed inside the car captured experienced drivers, Steve McQueen and Bud Ekins. McQueen won more than one race between the 1960s and 1970s, and Bud Ekins was one of Hollywood's best stunt drivers. The position of the rearview mirror is an indication of who was driving the car in each scene—when it's facing up, avoiding the driver's face, Ekins is behind the wheel.

7. c – Three; to date, Ford has introduced new versions of McQueen's GT in 2001, 2008, and 2019. The special edition Bullitt Mustangs offered the vintage look but with more horsepower. There have been several replicas from the original *Bullitt,* but none matched more closely than Dave Kunz's 1968 rendition which was used for Ford advertising purposes.

8. a – True; Denice Halicki holds the copyrights and trademarks to both *Gone in 60 Seconds* and *Eleanor*, as the vehicle appears in both versions of the film. She has gone on to create her own companies, Halicki films, and Eleanor Licensing and has been involved in several litigation suits over the years, protecting her rights to the movie franchise and *Eleanor*.

9. a – 1977 Cobra II; this second-generation Mustang made a lengthy appearance in the Eighties movie alongside actor Jeff Bridges. The alien clones a man and learns all about human ways, including how to drive a

1977 Cobra II as he travels across the US with the clone's widow.

10. b – Shelby GT500; Carroll Shelby jumped on the opportunity to make replica *Eleanors* based on the 2000 film *Gone in Sixty Second* and advertised them as such. This would prompt a lawsuit from Toby Halicki's widow, which was initially thrown out because Disney had actually held the rights to the silver car in the remake, which was markedly different than the yellow fastback from the 1974 movie. On appeals, Denice Halicki was able to win her lawsuit against Shelby and maintain that exclusive rights to any and all vehicles named *Eleanor* belonged to her.

11. d – *2 Fast 2 Furious;* 2003 was a big year for Saleen vehicles as the movies made it to Hollywood. *Bruce Almighty* also featured a Saleen vehicle that same year—an S7, as *God's car.* While the other 2 movies listed, *Fun with Dick and Jane* and *xXx: State of the Union,* also sported Saleen Mustangs, those films came out after 2003.

12. c – *War of the Worlds;* although all movies listed starred Tom Cruise, only *War of the Worlds* produced by Stephen Spielberg featured a 1966 Shelby GT 350H driven by Tom Cruise. The vehicle was own and upgraded by Gino Lucci of Picture Cars East.

13. a – Barricade; the Saleen S281 Police Car was present in three of the six movies, as well as a few comics.

14. c – *I Am Legend*; a 2007 adaptation of the 1954 horror novel, a lone Will Smith with his loyal dog in the seat next to him, drives a red 2007 Shelby GT500 around post-apocalyptic New York City.
15. a True; although only to a certain degree. In the 2008 film, the car Morgan Freeman drives is an exact replica of a 1966 Shelby GT 350. However, some internet sources indicate that the car was actually just a highly modified 1965 fastback, designed to look exactly like the Shelby Mustang. Sadly, the Shelby replica that is jumped off the dirt track at the very end was totaled after that stunt.
16. d – *Saxondale*; in the fictional tv series that only ran two seasons, the divorced and angry Tommy Saxondale probably treats his beloved Mach 1 better than anyone else in his life.
17. d – a & b; Filmmakers ordered seven of the SVT's first-generation stock mustangs to be transformed into a Super Snake and shipped to Bulgaria for filming. All seven Super Snakes were wrecked, some of them several times, and eventually, the parts made their way into 13 other Shelbys to finish filming. In all, crew members have reported that more than 130 vehicles were destroyed during the filming of *Getaway*. They even had to build their own nearby junkyard to accommodate the scraps.

18. b – 1967 2+2 Fastback 289; The Mustang plays a major role in the movie, and Roy comes back in 2 more films with his race car.

19. a – *Point Break*; in the 1991 film *Point Break*, Keanu Reeves drove a 1970 Mach 1, and 23 years later came back in *John Wick* to drive a 1969 Mach 1.

20. c – *Bullitt;* the infamous chase scene from the 1968 film, is playing on the Mt. Kisco's Drive-In theater screen as Tobey drives up in his 1969 Torino GT. Ironically, at the very end of *Need for Speed,* Ford's 50th anniversary Mustang gets a cameo on one of the same San Francisco streets where the *Bullitt*'s chase scene takes place.

Conclusion

The pony car market has grown, shrunk, and grown again over the last 55 plus years, and the landscape now, compared to a half-century ago, is vastly different. When anyone, anywhere in the world can buy a Mustang, or just about any other car, Ford knows it has to bring in that *something different*. Consider just the engines in the latest pony cars, and we're talking hundreds of horsepower of difference. The Fox body has gone away, and Mustangs rarely come with manual transmissions anymore, but that has not stopped Ford from offering performance on top of performance. As times change, priorities shift, and the competition evolves, so too has the Mustang.

The First-Generation Mustangs still lead in terms of sales, with the Third-Generation Fox body not too far behind. The Second Generation hardly deserves mention except that it eked out slightly more car sales than the Fifth-Generation Mustang, which struggled the most as they navigated the throes of America's deep recession. In another time, those *retro done right* Mustangs could have gone so much further. The decade of the Fourth-Generation Mustangs could be characterized as a *Mustang for everyone* (though some might argue it's closer to *everything but the kitchen sink*), with colors and options to satisfy a much broader market. The latest generation of Mustangs have given us the personality of its predecessors—along with a little OG Mustang DNA— and now all the performance and handling to match. Always looking forward, the Ford Motor Company has given Mustang fans everywhere just enough to eagerly anticipate what comes next.

CPSIA information can be obtained
at www.ICGtesting.com
Printed in the USA
BVHW040531221221
624596BV00017B/1709

9 781955 149006